Machiavelli

Machiavelli

A Portrait

CHRISTOPHER S. CELENZA

HARVARD UNIVERSITY PRESS

CAMBRIDGE, MASSACHUSETTS

LONDON, ENGLAND

2015

First printing

LIBRARY OF CONGRESS CATALOGING-IN-PUBLICATION DATA
IS AVAILABLE FROM THE LIBRARY OF CONGRESS.

ISBN: 978-0-674-41612-3

For Anna Harwell Celenza

Contents

Machiavelli

Prologue

Machiavelli. His name conjures up a vision of amoral conduct and the idea that the ends justify the means in everything from introductory political science classes to business manuals. These days he appears as a character in a wildly popular role-playing video game, *Assassin's Creed*, and he was a regular in Showtime's hit television series *The Borgias*. Pair the word "Machiavellian" with the name of almost any politician in an Internet search, and you will find a whole world of journalism to explore. Why are we so fascinated by him? Why has his name retained such a powerful hold on our imaginations?

The answer is found in *The Prince*, a short book he wrote in 1513. Though it was unprinted in his lifetime, *The Prince* went on to become an enduring bestseller, translated into numerous languages. Is it better to be loved or feared? How much does fortune influence human affairs? Should a leader be impetuous or measured? How do leaders plan for the future when there are always so many possible paths to take? How much do appearances matter? Machiavelli's answers to these and many other questions emerge in *The Prince*. It is the Italian Renaissance's most famous book, and it deserves the attention it has traditionally received. But it had a context. At first glance, the circumstances that led to the composition of *The Prince* seem almost unbelievable.

The year was 1512. Machiavelli, an active diplomat and political figure in Renaissance Florence, found himself and his city immersed in wars, tumultuous politics, and conspiracies. The Medici family had not been part of Florence's government since 1494. But after a good deal of back and forth, the Medici returned to Florence with Spanish backing. Machiavelli's name was discovered on a list of possible anti-Medici conspirators. He was arrested, imprisoned, and subjected to the *strappado*, that ingenious form of torture whereby your hands are tied behind your back, you are lifted up into the air by a rope on a pulley, and you are then dropped almost, but not quite, to the ground. At that final moment, the rope is jerked tight, and your arms almost come out of their sockets. Machiavelli was dropped six times.

Giovanni de' Medici, the son of Lorenzo the Magnificent, had been made a cardinal when he was a teenager. On March 9, 1513, he became pope. Amid the celebrations in Florence, an amnesty was declared, and the authorities released Machiavelli from prison on the condition that he remain in Florentine territory. So he went to a small family property in the countryside outside of Florence, and there he began to write what became *The Prince*.

Understood within the development of a life lived with such drama, as was Machiavelli's, with ups and downs that few of us could fathom or would want to consider, it is all the more impressive. And when we realize that Machiavelli's writings cover so much more than what is in *The Prince*—that he wrote histories, treatises on politics, even comedies, and that before

he wrote these works he had a substantial political and diplomatic career—we are propelled to find his origins, to see what
shaped him, to tell the story of his life. Only then can a clear
portrait emerge, a portrait that, like all such endeavors, must
be selective in order to communicate the essence of the subject.

I

Renaissance, Conspiracies, Bonfires

✦ ✦ ✦

If you are reading this book, you have probably never witnessed a public execution or been close to someone who has. Most likely, you have not been physically tortured during legal proceedings. And in all probability you don't live in a world where war is on your doorstep, literally, not outsourced and far away. Finally, in the course of your education, you were almost certainly not taught in a language that was neither your mother tongue nor a living language—but rather Latin. These are just some ways your world differs from that of Niccolò Machiavelli. The world you inhabit was not his world.

What was his world like? What did Machiavelli see, growing up in Florence? What did he learn? Why did Machiavelli express himself—in his language, style, and vocabulary—as he did? Biography, culture, and politics all played a role.

He was born in 1469 to Bernardo Machiavelli and Bartolomea de' Nelli. Bernardo possessed an advanced degree in law, and though not especially well off financially, he was a cultured man. Like many Florentines of his station, he kept a book of *Ricordi*—memories—as a way of documenting and preserving the major events in his life and those of his family.[1] From that book we learn that the young Machiavelli was sent to grammar school in 1476, where he learned some Latin as well as basic reading and writing in Tuscan. Then, in 1480, he learned the "abacus," which is the way Florentines of the time referred to basic mathematics, of the sort that was appropriate to a merchant society, such as Florence in the fifteenth century. The year 1481 saw young Niccolò placed under the tutelage of Paolo da Ronciglione, a teacher of Latin who, though little known today, counted a number of prominent Florentine intellectuals as his students.

In other words, Machiavelli had a solid early education, one that would have given him literacy as we know it: the basic ability to read and write one's own language. His education also made him, in the terms of his own era, *litteratus*, someone who had fluency in Latin. Latin mattered then, in ways that are difficult, if not impossible, to imagine today. For Machiavelli, as for those of his contemporaries who learned Latin, it provided a tool with which he could interpret the world as he experienced it.

◆ ◆ ◆

The Latin language had died out as a "native" language (one spoken naturally in the home to children, say) centuries earlier, as it was transformed into what scholars term "vulgar" Latin after the fall of the Roman Empire: Latin, but in a register more attuned to the sentence structure and vocabulary of the emerging Romance languages of Italian, French, and Spanish. The first written documentation of something recognizable as

Italian, as distinct from vulgar Latin, occurs only in the tenth century, in a manuscript preserving some legal formulas in southern Italy. Beautiful Italian poetry was written in the thirteenth century, as the poet Giacomo da Lentini penned works of courtly love at the southern Italian court of Frederick II, an admired ruler and cultural patron. Then, in the fourteenth century what Dante called his *Commedia*, or *Comedy* (later so admired that it came to be called the *Divine Comedy*) emerged as the Italian language's great, foundational literary monument.

The exemplary beauty and linguistic limpidity of the *Comedy* served as an important model. Almost two centuries after its composition, during Machiavelli's lifetime, in the 1520s in fact, Italian thinkers who desired to draw up rules of grammar and vocabulary for the Italian language, picking among the various Italian dialects, chose Tuscan, the language of the *Comedy*, as their basis. The hope of these language experts was to mold Italian in such a way that it would be seen as appropriate for serious works of literature, history, and philosophy. As we shall see, Machiavelli did not have *The Prince* printed—officially "published"—in this lifetime. But he did circulate it in handwritten, or "manuscript," form. And it is a curious fact that one of the reasons that the earliest readers of *The Prince* admired it was its use of a seemingly perfect Tuscan. Again, we ask: how could a native language *not* be seen as a legitimate vehicle for meaningful work? Why was Italian not seen, intuitively, as a language in which it was possible to write durable, permanent works? The answer to these questions brings us back, again, to Latin. Examining its history in the Middle Ages and then in the century into which Machiavelli was born allows us to begin to paint a picture of Machiavelli in the round, to see where and how he was traditional, where he was unique, and where he was a product of his times.

Just as the Roman Empire went into decline—and decline there was, this is inarguable: far less trade took place across the vast territories from Africa to Britain, the idea of central civil governance practically collapsed, and obvious declines took place from previously higher standards of literacy—the Christian Church experienced growth and centralization in a manner that in retrospect seems preordained. It would not have seemed so then, of course: even as late as the sixth century AD, there were many people in the Mediterranean region who practiced other faiths. And it is certainly true that, as the saying goes, "history is written by the victors," and that those early Christians who created the written record emphasized and indeed created the narrative of inevitability. But a line can be drawn from the era of Constantine, the first Christian Roman emperor, active in the early fourth century, through the epoch of Theodosius in the latter part of that century, and finally through the fifth century, that saw the church working through controversies by means of church councils and creating an ever more centralized orthodox doctrine through the writings of its most prominent thinkers.

Early Christian church fathers like Jerome, Ambrose, Augustine (all active in the late fourth and early fifth centuries AD), and, later, Gregory (pope from 590 to 604), created what turned out to be lasting visions of the Christian religion. Jerome had been heavily involved in translating the New Testament, written originally in Greek, into Latin. Ambrose wrote various works in which he assimilated aspects of ancient Roman culture into emerging Christianity (even going so far as to pen a Christian version of Cicero's classic work of Stoic philosophy *On Duties*). And in his *Confessions* and *City of God*, Augustine provided a personal conversion narrative and a Christian scheme of history that became and remained touchstones thereafter. In his numerous other works, Augustine addressed and, in his own view, resolved many problems and questions that arose regarding how to reconcile the many competing ideas that the Christian faith needed to address: What was the nature of the Trinity? How could God have created something out of nothing? How do Christians incorporate pagan learning, with all of its literary and philosophical monuments from Plato to Virgil, into their own worldview? Augustine's writings and those of other early Christian thinkers provided relatively uniform answers to these and many other questions. As we shall see, the nature of the premodern world was such that no attempt in theory could ever succeed fully in practice: local forms of Christianity persisted all through the Middle Ages, often slightly (and sometimes more so) at odds with what the orthodox vision of Christianity seemed to be.

Important, however, is the language in which those church fathers wrote: Latin. What this meant was that the Christian Church fostered the Latin language, boasted acknowledged "classics" in the writings of the church fathers by the early Middle Ages (let us say by the year 750 AD), and adopted the Latin language as its own. Latin became the language of the church and, since so much education was connected with the church, the language of education as well. Yet it is clear that by the early eighth century in Europe, vernaculars had emerged, some of which had grown out of Latin, and that the knowledge of classical Latin had weakened. Thinkers around the court of

Charlemagne, the Franco-German ruler who created the origins of the geography of modern Europe, saw the decline in Latin as a serious matter and one that could harm Christianity. One of these thinkers, the English cleric Alcuin, engaged, along with his colleagues in a reform campaign, in both collating scriptural texts to try to remove inconsistencies (inevitable in a world of handwritten books) and creating manuals and simple dialogues to teach Latin consistently. To some extent, this reform was successful, as ever more standardized versions of scripture began to circulate and minimum standards of Latin learning for clergy rose.

By the eleventh century, Europe's decline had begun to reverse itself: towns revived, trade and commerce increased, and the stage was set for a flowering of learning in the twelfth century. The works of Aristotle, the ancient Greek philosopher and student of Plato, began to be translated into Latin and became the basis for serious study. Scholars like Peter Abelard, whose account of his tragic affair with his student Eloise continues to inspire great emotion, gained fame and groups of students who followed them. When a large enough number of scholars gathered into one place, concentrated centers of learning developed in areas of certain cities, like the left bank of the Seine in Paris. It was there, in the early thirteenth century, that one of the earliest universities took firm root, the University of Paris. Elsewhere in Europe—in Oxford, Bologna, Salerno, and Naples, just to name a few cities—universities became centers of higher learning.

At all of them, Latin was the common language: classes were taught in Latin, all texts to be studied were written in Latin (or, as in the case of Aristotle, translated into Latin), and students were expected to be proficient in the language. These early universities were cosmopolitan and exciting centers to which students traveled who wanted advanced training. A student would study grammar (which included much Latin literature) and logic (drawn from Aristotle) for up to six years in the "arts" faculty and arrive at the status of *baccalaureus artium* (a "bachelor of arts," the distant origins of our bachelor's degree). Thereafter the student could eventually enter one of the three "higher" faculties of theology, medicine, and law. Certain universities developed specialties: Paris for theology, Bologna for law, Salerno for medicine.

The fourteenth century saw more universities emerge and the development of relatively standardized curricula in the arts faculties. The proliferation of universities meant that students had less need to travel great distances to study a certain specialty. And this standardization and opening of opportunities for study proved professionally advantageous. But standardized curricula and a more local character also meant conservatism, in the most literal sense: preserving what has gone before. This useful function of all higher education is important, as tried and true methods and conclusions in many different fields endure. Yet at times those outside of the university world may come to believe that the methods and subjects cultivated inside universities (with the hyperspecialization and inside baseball that ensue) are not relevant to life outside the university. The fourteenth century was one of those times, as thinkers from both within and without universities raised voices of protest, sometimes exaggerated, against the sorts of learning, styles of thought, and types of Latin that had gained footholds. Within the context of universities one saw a figure like Jean Gerson, who served as chancellor of the University of Paris, argue that forms of writing needed to be cultivated that addressed problems relevant to public life.[2]

In Italy, a movement developed that later scholars would term Renaissance humanism. The Tuscan thinker Petrarch (who spent much of his life in southern France) was the most prominent fourteenth-century humanist. Though Petrarch is known today more for his vernacular love poetry, in his own lifetime he was intent on recapturing a seemingly lost ancient Roman world, doing so first and foremost by the study and use of the Latin language. Like late medieval Italian thinkers before him, Petrarch drew inspiration from classical Latin, from the era that produced the great Roman orator Cicero, the powerful ancient historian Livy, and the poet Virgil, whose enduring monument, the *Aeneid*, told in twelve books the mythical story of Rome's foundation in a language both beautiful and profound. Petrarch's connection to these and other works was deeply intimate. To his friend, Giovanni Boccaccio, author of the ribald Italian collection of tales *The Decameron*, Petrarch wrote that he read certain ancient texts so often and so deeply, that they entered the marrow of his bones, and that he had internalized them to such an extent that he at times could not even distinguish where an ancient author's thought left off and his own began.[3]

Petrarch was a sensitive soul, perhaps too much so. He wrote letters to his ancient heroes, long since dead of course, lamenting the sorry state of the world in which he found himself, the loss of ancient glory, and the low state of politics in his day. In the chapter library of a church in Verona, Petrarch discovered the ancient orator Cicero's *Letters to Atticus*, in which Cicero revealed himself as a gossipy politician rather than as the Stoic sage whom Petrarch's contemporaries had imagined. Disappointed that his hero was all too human, Petrarch chastised Cicero in 1345—in other words from almost a millennium and a half's distance in time—for having been too political and not philosophical enough: "These failings fill my heart with pity and shame . . . what does it profit a man, I ask, to teach others virtue, going on and on, if he fails to follow his own instructions? . . . Farewell forever, my Cicero. From the land of the living."[4] *Relax, Petrarch,* you almost want to say. Yet he did sign these letters "from the land of the living" and, unlike the ancient pagan authors he prized, he was deeply Christian and attentive to the lamentable condition of the church. Petrarch, in short, devoted himself to ancient writers with his whole heart, but he always kept an eye on the world in which he lived. Studying those ancient Latin works intensively as he did, Petrarch recognized something important: that the Latin with which he and other thinkers were surrounded, in universities and in the church, did not correspond in register, diction, and syntax to the ancient Latin he loved so well.

Petrarch and others like him studied ancient Latin works ever more intensively, they compared differing manuscripts of the "same" text, and they traveled far and wide to search for ancient Latin texts that had been lost to the Middle Ages. Given these factors, it was inevitable that they would come to some fundamentally different ideas regarding history from those who immediately preceded them. They began to see that ancient authorities, though venerable, were all, themselves, figures in time, with their own historical context. For Dante, Aristotle had been "the master of those who know."[5] For Renaissance humanists

Aristotle became one of a number of possible ancient masters, all of whom needed attention and study.

Fifteenth-century thinkers even researched the history of the ancient Latin language. Petrarch and his immediate predecessors were heirs of the medieval idea that Latin was in a sense a "timeless" language, an unchanging language of craft and rules that needed schools to teach it.[6] Yet the more that fifteenth-century thinkers like Leonardo Bruni, Poggio Bracciolini, and Biondo Flavio studied the problem, the more they realized that ancient Latin had been a "natural" language, one spoken in the home. Discoveries of hitherto unknown texts fueled research and vice versa. Around 1420, for example, humanists rediscovered a dialogue of Cicero lost to the Middle Ages, called *Brutus*. In it Cicero presents lively portraits of renowned speakers of his own day, offering anecdotes about them and assessments of their abilities. One of them, Curio, was said to have been the third-best speaker in the city of Rome, even though he had no formal education. How, Cicero's avid fifteenth-century readers wondered, could he have become an expert in this timeless language without any education, since present-day thinkers needed years of education to master the language?

Here is another instance: fifteenth-century thinkers studied another great ancient master of oratory, Quintilian, who wrote a guide to educating the young. He made sure to say that parents should hire nursemaids who spoke Latin well.[7] Again, the implication was that in the ancient world there was not a separate vernacular, like Italian, alongside another "high" language, Latin, requiring formal education. The humanists who preceded Machiavelli studied ancient Latin so intensively that they came to the conclusion, without saying so in so many words, that Latin was a "dead" language. Yet as Machiavelli reached maturity, this historical acuity also allowed Renaissance humanists to transform Latin. It still needed to be used as a common language for diplomacy, the church, and education. By the end of the fifteenth century, the right way to write Latin was in classical cadences, imitating the structure of Cicero's prose. Writers and scholars had changed elite language—then the only international language—by studying the past.

It would contradict too much available evidence to say, as earlier scholars have done, that the Italian Renaissance was a great revolution of the human spirit and that Italian Renaissance men were, as the nineteenth-century scholar Jacob Burckhardt put it, "the first-born among the sons of modern Europe."[8] All of them lived in a profoundly "premodern" world, as we shall see. Still, discoveries of ancient texts hitherto unknown, intense critical study of those texts, and the consequences that ensued, including, among some humanists, a different view of history and language: these are undeniable features of the Italian Renaissance. They form part of the world that Machiavelli inherited: Latinate, attentive to the power and importance of ancient examples in shaping modern life, and historically acute.

◆ ◆ ◆

We left Machiavelli in 1481, as he was placed in the care of a respected teacher. It is a curious fact that, after Machiavelli's early education, he disappears almost entirely from the historical record until 1498—especially curious, since Florence is, on balance, one of late medieval Europe's most well documented cities. But at least we can trace what Machiavelli experienced, directly or indirectly, as he came to maturity. If one of those experiences consisted in inheriting a rich literary and historical culture, as did all of his literate contemporaries, another, certainly, would have been the simple fact of growing up in Florence.

Italy's greatest strength in the high Middle Ages came from its vigorously independent city-states. Venice, Milan, the Papal States, Naples, and Florence—often in alliances with one another, many times bringing foreign powers into the picture—all served as centers of culture, intrigue, and political dynamism. Florence was distinguished, in the late Middle Ages, by its mercantile interests, wherein banking and the cloth trade served to make some of its citizens among the wealthiest in Europe. Nominally Florence was a "republic," meaning that all eligible citizens had the right to vote and participate in government. While nothing like the drive toward universal enfranchisement that is prized today, this republicanism was important to elite Florentines and served as one of its distinguishing markers. Property-holding males with a number of years of residency could participate in government (usually this number was around twenty years, though the laws regulating it frequently changed). The elegant Palazzo Vecchio (or Palazzo della Signoria), aside from the Duomo Florence's most distinctive architectural landmark, hosted twelve citizens for two months at a time. Chosen by lot, they lived and legislated within that imposing structure, to cede their place to the next group of twelve when their term was up. No political system works perfectly: the "lots" were often manipulated, family and kinship structures mattered greatly, and, in every decade of the fifteenth century, there was always intrigue. Still, especially (and unsurprisingly) whenever the city was under attack, its leaders rallied around the flag of the "republic," invoking (as sources from the Florentine archives show) what they called their *libertà*, or "freedom."[9]

The fifteenth century saw a great concentration of wealth and political power in the hands of the Medici family, especially from the early 1430s onward. Cosimo de' Medici, the victim of local political intrigue by rival families, returned to Florence in 1434 after spending a year in exile, and thereafter the Medici consolidated their power. Cosimo's riches allowed him to become Florence's leading arts and culture patron. Cosimo convinced leaders of the church to move an important church council to Florence in 1439, the last attempt, as it turned out, to unify the western and eastern branches of the Christian Church. Numerous institutions benefited from or were created by his largesse. The remodeling of the church of San Lorenzo, with its original design by Brunelleschi and later with work by Michelozzo; the famous library of the Dominican church of San Marco (arguably the first "public" library of the Italian Renaissance); and of course the Medici Palace itself, on the via Larga (what is today via Cavour), a prototypical Italian Renaissance building with its rough crenellated stone on the outside projecting power and, on the inside and reflecting refinement, some of Europe's finest works of art: these monuments and many more served as a sign of Medici power, as possible expiation for a wealthy banker always afraid the interest rates he charged might amount to usury and, ultimately, as validation of what much of Italy realized—that Florence had become, by the middle of the fifteenth century, Italy's premier center of culture.

These were the years of Donatello, whose lithe David brought back realistic sculpture of the full human form, of Brunelleschi, whose spectacular dome capped off Florence's cathedral in a manner that left contemporaries wonderstruck, and of Lorenzo Ghiberti, whose bronze doors to Florence's age-old baptistery, where Dante himself had been baptized, proved so entrancing and long-lived that Michelangelo later termed them the "Gates of Paradise." The Dominican friar Fra Angelico created frescoes for the cells of the friars who lived at San Marco, each one as much a distilled scriptural message as an object of profound meditation. Paolo Uccello became one of the first painters of the Renaissance fully to appreciate and to employ the lost techniques of perspective, the art of making a two-dimensional surface seem three-dimensional to a viewer, by representing objects smaller as they appear to recede into the distance. And then, of course, there was Sandro Botticelli. His famous paintings, the *Primavera* (his great allegory of spring) and the *Birth of Venus* (his representation of the mythical birth of the goddess of love) have today been mass reproduced in so many ways that it is difficult to recover the excitement they produced in the 1480s, when Botticelli created them—how new they seemed, how delicate, how sensual. These cultural monuments and more all emerged during the central decades of the fifteenth century, when the star of the Medici family seemed ever in the ascendant.

History, however, always seems clearer in retrospect than it does on the ground. Though the fifteenth century in Florence seems to have been the "age of the Medici" and though we find no shortage of contemporaries from that epoch who praised Medici influence, nonetheless every decade saw challenges to

Medici power: attempts at political coups and barely foiled conspiracies dotted the decades of Medici rule. Critics whispered, as the century wore on, that the Medici behaved more like *signori*, entitled nobility accustomed to one-man rule, than like members of a republic. And the social cues that Italy's *signori* cultivated—lavish public festivals featuring family members and a general taste for public opulence—had their place in Medici Florence, especially during the ascendancy of Lorenzo the Magnificent, Cosimo's grandson, who found himself at the helm of the Medici ship at the young age of twenty in 1469, the very year of Machiavelli's birth. Cosimo upon his death in 1464 had been declared *pater patriae,* "father of the homeland," and was considered during his lifetime *primus inter pares,* "first among equals." His grandson Lorenzo soon began to seem less like the first among equals and more like a prince.

Lorenzo's career in the Florence of Machiavelli's youth became the basis for legends and myths of a golden age. And just as in many other myths and legends, there was a foundation in fact. Lorenzo took the lead in refounding Florence's university in 1473, leading a campaign to hire the best professors in law at the university's main branch, in Florence's gateway to the sea, Pisa. In Florence itself, where the humanities were taught, some of the best scholars of the day gathered, including by the 1480s the best of the best, Angelo Poliziano, whose work Machiavelli would come to know and use. Poliziano when quite young, at the age of sixteen, had so impressed Lorenzo with a translation into Latin of parts of Homer's *Iliad* (the foundational Greek epic telling the story of the Trojan War) that Lorenzo took Poliziano into the Medici household, laying the foundations for a lifelong friendship.

Poliziano was in Florence in 1478, as was the young Machiavelli, when the most dramatic event of Lorenzo's life occurred: a conspiracy, led by a rival family in Florence, the Pazzi, to murder Lorenzo the Magnificent and his brother Giuliano. One key source we have for this conspiracy is, in fact, Poliziano's own account, written in Latin, called *Commentary on the Pazzi Conspiracy*, which tells us so much about the world in which Machiavelli grew up—about people's basic assumptions, about politics, and about the ever-present potential for public violence of a high order—that it is worth pausing over. What do we learn about this violent event, one that Machiavelli himself would treat much later, when he undertook to write his own history of Florence?

It was planned for Sunday, April 26, 1478, the Sunday before Ascension Day. The fact that the conspirators planned the event soon before the feast day commemorating Christ's ascension into heaven would have proved bitterly ironic, had they succeeded fully in their plans. What they did accomplish was bad enough. As the priest raised the host, during the most solemn moment of the Mass, one of the Pazzi family, Francesco, aided by a fellow-conspirator, Bernardo Bandini, as well as others, surrounded Lorenzo's brother, Giuliano. Bernardo struck the severest blow, and Francesco, inflamed by hatred, stabbed Giuliano numerous times. Others attacked Lorenzo but he escaped with only light wounds, retreating into the sacristy with the aid of a faithful friend who died protecting Lorenzo. "Then I," Poliziano tells us, "who had withdrawn to the same place with some others, shut the bronze doors."[10]

Lorenzo made it to safety, and Poliziano, with more eyewitness testimony, informs us: "I went straight to the house by the shortest route and came across Giuliano's body wretchedly lying there, fouled with the blood of many wounds." The conspirators had overestimated the extent of anti-Medici sentiment in Florence. They attempted to rally support, even going so far as to attempt to occupy the Palazzo Vecchio, Florence's hallowed seat of government. Thereafter, Florentine citizens and Medici supporters rounded up the conspirators near and far, and the Palazzo Vecchio played yet another important role, as a site of public, retributive violence: "They hung Jacopo dei Poggi from the windows; they led the captive cardinal [Raffaele Riario, 1461–1521, made a Cardinal at age 16] to the Palazzo with a large guard and had much difficulty in protecting him from an attack by the people. Most of those who followed him were killed by the crowd, all torn apart, their bodies mangled cruelly; in front of Lorenzo's doors someone brought, now a head fixed on a spear, now a shoulder." And then: "From the same window as Francesco Pazzi, the archbishop of Pisa was also hung directly above the dead body itself. When he had been cut down (I witnessed in the amazed faces of the crowd what happened, and it was unknown to none at the time), either by chance or anger he bit Francesco's corpse in the chest, and even as he was strangled by the noose, his eyes wide open in rage, he hung onto it with his teeth. After this the necks of the two Jacopos Salviati were broken by hanging."[11]

Some conspirators escaped Florence, but they were eventually found and brought to brutal justice: "The people mutilated them horribly; they cut off their noses and their ears, hacked at them with many blows, and, after they had made their confession to the crime, the criminals were carried off to the gallows. . . . [T]here followed many killings." Giuliano's funeral was held in the Medici Church of San Lorenzo. Giuliano was twenty-five at the time of his death. This flower of Florentine youth had earned the city's admiration a few years back by his gallant performance in a public joust. Poliziano tells us: "he had been pierced with nineteen wounds."[12]

Soon after the event Florence was troubled by what seemed like unseasonable rains. People wound up blaming it on the fact that Jacopo Pazzi, another conspirator and member of the notorious family, was buried within the walls. The Florentines dug him up and buried him outside the walls. Some Florentine boys, hearing of this reburial, then dug Jacopo up yet again, dragging him all over Florence, cutting up his corpse, and even kicking around his head as if it were a ball. Meditating on the entire affair (the conspiracy, the tumultuous events it engendered, and the terrible consequences) Poliziano writes: "From this great upheaval of human affairs I am directly warned about the fickleness of human affairs."[13]

This detailed account of the Pazzi conspiracy is in numerous ways a Renaissance-era set piece. Like many of his fellow intellectuals, Poliziano believed he needed ancient models when he wrote. And he had one here, in *The Conspiracy of Catiline*, the ancient Roman historian Sallust's memorable account of a conspiracy that the Roman figure Catiline had enacted against Julius Caesar. Poliziano does take some of his cues from his model: the conspirators are not complex human beings with interlocking webs of motivation. Instead they are pure evil from head to toe, sniveling, cowardly, and unappreciative of the time in which they live, blessed as it seemed to be under the watchful eyes of the Medici. The Medici by contrast are unremittingly blameless—steadfast pillars of Florentine society who represent the ultimate source of good government and high culture. Despite the tragedy of losing Giuliano, in the end order is restored, sealed in a classic premodern way by gruesome but inevitable acts of violence, in a sequence that is as old as Homer's *Odyssey*. There the hero Odysseus, after years of wandering, adventures, and yearning for home, brutally slaughters those men who had been frequenting his home, trying to win the affections of his wife, Penelope, who had patiently and faithfully awaited the return of her husband.

So in one sense Poliziano is following a script. Still, his treatise represents the closest we can get to an eyewitness account. And, in any case, plausibility to contemporaries is as important as the unvarnished truth. In other words, on the surface there is a narrative of many different specific events, each one of which might have different possible interpretations, according to the assumptions of the observer. But underneath the surface, Poliziano's account reveals a lot about the basic, taken for granted assumptions of his society—and Machiavelli's.

What do we learn? First, it was an age of conspiracies and a time and place where government was "close."[14] How many citizens, today, have direct contact with the real powers that be in our society? After the industrial revolution and the development of large sovereign states with equally large and ever-expanding governments, the modern world puts the institutions of government far away from most of us. In Machiavelli's Florence, however, a citizen was likely to see and to know those who governed, to be enmeshed in an extended web of kinship ties with some of them—or to feel resentment at not being part of whatever larger kinship group currently did hold power. There were no mass transit, no mass circulation of ideas through newspapers, and no significant novels with long arcs of character development, through which one could learn about the emotions—and the common humanity—of people one had never met. It was a premodern world, in other words, despite the remarkable culture that arose in the fifteenth century.

These premodern conditions also meant that public violence was close to home, visible, and, from our modern western perspective, common. A citizen growing up in fifteenth-century Florence would have seen public executions and other forms of ritual violence (such as the public hangings after the conspiracy), despite Florence's status as an acknowledged European cultural capital. Vendettas were common. There were no universally agreed upon theories of human rights (in the style of "life, liberty, and the pursuit of happiness") that later ages in the west would take for granted—imperfectly pursued as those rights have often been. The existence of public, retributive violence was a given. How one used it was the question, a question to which Machiavelli returns again and again.

Beyond violence, another characteristic of this world was its deeply premodern religious nature. Poliziano is serious when he writes that people dug up Jacopo Pazzi's body because they believed that his burial location, within the Florentine walls, could have been causing excessive and abnormal rain. And such beliefs were not confined to the uneducated. From low to high, Machiavelli's world was one in which what would today seem superstitions were taken for granted: before experimental science, many of the most reputable intellectuals believed in the real existence of demons, mystical correspondences between the heavens and the earth, and what would today seem the wilder reaches of folk medicine. This, then, was the world in which

Machiavelli came of age, a world in which the highest forms of learning and scholarship existed alongside beliefs that seem incompatible to our modern eyes but that, to people then—high and low, wealthy and poor—seemed so self-evident that they often did not need to be articulated.

Machiavelli and others must have marveled at Lorenzo's continued success and dynamism after the assassination attempt. Lorenzo made what seemed a daring voyage to Naples, to negotiate a peace agreement with the leadership of that state. He continued his patronage of the arts and humanities, as well as the writing of his own Italian poetry, in its most famous lines prefiguring what Castiglione in his *Courtier* would, a few short decades later, call *sprezzatura*, meaning an attitude toward life that included intelligence, physical grace, and a sense that one made it all look easy: *chi vuol'essere lieto, sia: di doman non c'è certezza*—"be happy if you wish, for tomorrow promises nothing certain."[15]

When Lorenzo died in 1492, bitter proof of the truth of those lines—of the instability of the world and the mutability of human circumstances—emerged with astonishing rapidity. Within a few short years, everything seemed to change in Florence, against a backdrop of much larger changes in the political situation in Europe. For Italy especially, its greatest strength in the Middle Ages, its strong, stubbornly independent city-states, became its greatest weakness as France, Spain, and England came into their own as powerful sovereign states, much larger in their size, political ambitions, and eventual centralization of power. Italy's city-states became coveted allies, prey, and sometimes little more than gambling chips among these larger emerging nations and the games they played.

In retrospect, this development represents a bitter irony, for it was Italy above all, especially its northern and central states, that had taught medieval Europe the art of politics, both monarchical and republican. Cities such as Milan, Venice, Genoa, and Florence, not to mention smaller but equally proud cities like Ferrara, Mantua, Siena, Pisa, and Lucca, had, in the eleventh and twelfth centuries, liberated themselves from the creaky, faraway vestiges of early medieval papal or imperial rule, declaring their independence and creating institutions of governance that resonated for centuries to come. Some, like Venice and Florence, stayed republics, and others, such as Milan and Ferrara, became ruled by hereditary families. And, of course, there were intrigues, wars, and vacillations in forms of governance among these entrepreneurial "city-states," not quite big enough to be called nations, but more all-encompassing in their ambitions and reach—each with its own foreign policy, unique currency, and characteristic dialect—than the term "city" suggests.

But size matters, as does military force. As France, Spain, and England consolidated power in the late fifteenth and sixteenth centuries, the independence of the Italian city-states faded. Each had its own story, and each story inspired reflection among intellectuals, none more so than that of Florence.

For Florence, the 1490s represented the beginning of what Machiavelli and many others would term the "ruin" of Italy. It was believed that portents accompanied Lorenzo the Magnificent's death in 1492, according to contemporary accounts, later memorialized by Machiavelli and other prominent intellectuals. A few days before Lorenzo died, when he was gravely ill, lightning struck the Duomo. When he died, wolves were said to howl, eerie screams resounded, and a woman was heard shrieking, in one of Florence's two Dominican churches, that a bull with fiery horns was destroying the city. The accounts of these episodes indicate that contemporaries believed Lorenzo had been a momentous figure. As these seeming portents added up in the days, weeks, months, and years that followed they were also colored by the seemingly disastrous developments in Florentine life and politics that occurred soon thereafter; the "age of Lorenzo" was memorialized against a backdrop of increasing disorder.[16]

As head of the Medici party and family, Lorenzo's son Piero lacked his father's cunning, charm, and political agility. Even in the best of times, there was opposition to Medici power, and once Lorenzo was gone, the volume of those voices of protest rose. So it was that in 1494, Florence saw the political ascendancy of a Dominican preacher from Ferrara, Girolamo Savonarola, whose prominence in Florence lasted for four years.[17]

Savonarola's appeal to Florentines lay in his religious fervor and his politics. Savonarola's preaching—apocalyptically oriented, rich with biblical parallels, and full of prophecy—earned him a following in an era when public preaching was a form of mass entertainment. Before his real rise to power, he preached that a conqueror would come from the north, like a "new Cyrus," evoking the ancient military leader who had established the largest ancient empire, that of the Persians (as the great ancient Greek historian Herodotus and other sources had recounted). When the French king, Charles VIII, crossed the Alps aiming to increase French dominion by pressing his ancestral claim to Naples and Sicily, people stood up and noticed. Greater concern emerged when Piero de' Medici, Lorenzo's hapless son, seemed to offer no resistance to the French as they made their way through Florentine domains, even surrendering, almost solely on his own authority, a series of fortresses in Florentine territories to French control. Savonarola's response was, essentially, that the Florentines had it coming, given over to luxury as they were and having lost touch with their ancient traditions of republican governance.

The Dominican Order assigned Savonarola to the church of San Marco in Florence, whose convent Fra Angelico had recently adorned with a series of frescoes. Savonarola's audience grew so large that he needed to move to the cathedral, the Duomo. Taking biblical texts such as the Gospel of John and the Book of Revelation as his basis, he preached against clerical corruption, against unwarranted consumption, against excessively sensual art with non-Christian themes, and against the Renaissance's love of pagan literature. Famously Savonarola substituted traditionally raucous carnival celebrations with a grim "Bonfire of the Vanities," in which seemingly scandalous carnival clothing, profane books, and works of art were gathered, placed on a pyre, and burned. As in the case of many such controversial events, pro- and anti-Savonarola partisans had different versions of what precisely happened, even if the larger symbolic importance of the Bonfire remained potent.

It was the events of 1494, however—the arrival of the French, the dissatisfaction of many Florentines with Piero de' Medici, Piero's subsequent expulsion from Florence, and the immediate inability of Florence's small political class to come up with a satisfactory government—that allowed Savonarola to cross over into a more political landscape. It was dangerous territory, as he would discover. He had gained prominence in the city by then, having led a delegation to the French king, urging Charles to spare Florence. After the French left, Savonarola took a lead role in Florentine politics. His followers were known as the *frateschi*—those who adhered to the *frate* or "friar." They were also mocked as *piagnoni* or "whiners," a name first hurled at them in opprobrium, which they subsequently adopted as their own. Employing the always politically powerful myth of a golden age, Savonarola recalled in his public preaching a former age of republican greatness, in which many of Florence's regular citizens had been more enfranchised, with political offices more widely distributed. As they merged religion and politics, Savonarola and his party reformed Florentine government, enlarging the parliament and making more offices open to larger proportions of citizens.

This political change proved so powerful that Savonarola and Florence were soon making news in Italy's various corridors of power, most notably at the Vatican. Savonarola was called to Rome to meet the pope, the savvy but morally dissolute Spaniard, Alexander VI, formerly Rodrigo Borgia. The pope offered Savonarola elevation to the cardinalate. Savonarola responded that instead of a red cardinal's hat, he would prefer a hat red with blood, unknowingly foreshadowing his later fate. Like the Medici before him, Savonarola did not have a unified Florence behind him, and as papal pressure increased, the voices of dissent increased as well—primarily the voices of disenfranchised oligarchs as well as those of a more secular bent, who, though they considered themselves good Christians, nonetheless appreciated ancient literature and the new art of the Renaissance, considering Savonarola a fanatical, antirational extremist.

The voices grew so loud that the tide turned. The pope excommunicated Savonarola on May 12, 1497, informing the Florentine government that the city would be placed under interdict if the friar were allowed continued influence. Savonarola was persuaded to stop public preaching for the good of the republic, retiring to his cell. Yet he continued to believe in himself as a prophet sent by God, and he was probably sincere in the hints he gave that miracles would occur to prove his divine mission. So when one of his most fanatical followers agreed to a challenge from a rival religious order in the form of a public trial by fire, Savonarola could not say no. The existence of this "trial by fire"—the notion that a large crowd would turn out, as indeed it did, to see if the Lord would protect a person walking though fire and miraculously prevent him from being burned alive—again highlights the instability of Florence in those days, as well as its premodern character. And when the trial was cancelled because of sudden violent rains (and, probably, last-minute jitters), tensions rose.

The next day, Palm Sunday 1498, crowds stormed San Marco, Savonarola's home. Soon thereafter, he and his two primary Dominican followers were arrested there on the charge of having incited public disturbances. Under torture, Savonarola confessed that he had invented his prophecies, retracted once, then confessed again. Imprisoned by that point in the highest point of Florence's Palazzo Vecchio—the symbolic center of political Florence and along with the Duomo the city's most recognizable monument—he was, finally, led down with his two followers to the square over which that building towers. Three gallows had been erected with kindling at their lowest points.

Stripped of his Dominican garb he was hanged, as were the other two, their bodies burned thereafter and their ashes cast into Florence's river Arno, so that pious followers would not be tempted to take them as relics.

What was Machiavelli thinking, then almost thirty years old, as these tumultuous events occurred and as this combination of religion and politics exploded into events such as Florence had never seen? He tells us only later in his written works. At the moment, in 1498, he was poised to enter into the most exciting phase of his life.

2

Highs and Lows

MACHIAVELLI EMERGES

✦   ✦   ✦

After Savonarola's execution, the continuing project of governing the city fell back to Florence's ruling elite, those who through wealth, influence, and family ties had leading roles in the city's governance. One of these men was Piero Soderini, who would turn out to be one of Florence's most important and most controversial leaders. A member of a distinguished Florentine family, Soderini counted among his kin a brother who was a cardinal and another who had been a Savonarola supporter. Soderini served as Florence's ambassador to France in 1493, during Piero de' Medici's ill-starred ascendancy. Soderini, along with like-minded supporters, took the lead in forming a government with new and, they hoped, more balanced approaches in mind. If Savonarola's governmental reforms had opened the republic up somewhat to allow a larger proportion of people to participate in office-holding, Soderini and his cohort believed that the pendulum should swing back a bit. They hoped to put Florence's affairs back in the hands of a smaller, tighter governing coalition, all committed to Florentine *libertà*—"liberty," that classic word that Florentines all used to describe their ideal government. The rub, as always, lay in the question of what liberty meant. Was it freedom from foreign domination? This, for the most part, is how Machiavelli would come to construe things. But if the liberty of self-government was at issue, then the question became: Liberty for whom? And how? Soderini and his allies worked out answers to these questions that, in the constantly evolving landscape of Florentine life, changed shape repeatedly.

By 1502 Soderini had become Florence's chief standard-bearer, or *gonfaloniere*, with one big change: traditionally this position of power, both real and symbolic, had been held for two months at a time, by one of the nine representatives who lived and governed in the Palazzo della Signoria. These "Priors" had to be members of Florence's various craft guilds, and they were chosen to represent the different neighborhoods of Florence. (Membership could be pro forma: Dante, for example, had joined the guild of doctors and apothecaries so that he could participate in the Florentine government, though he had no special expertise in those realms.) One prior would serve as the government's de facto head, with the title *gonfaloniere* of justice. The two-month tenure of the priors and *gonfaloniere* of justice meant, first, that there was a great deal of turnover and, second, that a relatively substantial number of male members of Florence's ruling class would have a chance to serve in some capacity at some point in their lives. Soderini by contrast was named *gonfaloniere a vita*, "for life," an anomalous-seeming designation in a Florence that, even during the Medici consolidation of power, always respected the appearance of this guild-based republican form of government that went back to the late thirteenth century. So the potential for explosiveness was built into the very governmental structure Machiavelli inhabited. This sense of the instability of governmental life never left him, and it made its way into everything he later wrote.

Even before Soderini took his lifetime office, he and his followers tapped the young Machiavelli for two important offices in 1498. The first was the secretary to a governmental body called the Second Chancery, which normally considered internal policy as well as matters related to war. Soon thereafter its functioning was merged with another governmental organ, called the Ten of Liberty and Peace, known as The Ten. This committee had primary responsibilities for maintaining relations with Florence's ambassadors. As such, it had a large share, not so much in making foreign policy, but in providing the information on which policy could be made. These years became the happiest of Machiavelli's life and the most active, as Florence sent him on repeated missions to meet with the city's friends and enemies. Machiavelli accompanied official ambassadors (who, again, were drawn from Florence's elite), drafting and sending home perspicacious accounts of what happened in their meetings and negotiations with foreign— non-Florentine—rulers, military captains, and royalty. His Latin title, *secretarius florentinus*, "Florentine secretary," represented much of what he prized about his life during this period: the ability to write incisively, clearly, and effectively about matters of politics and war, the association with his home city, and the ability and obligation to make recommendations that the city's leaders often followed.

During the first decade of the sixteenth century, Machiavelli saw and did much that shaped his views of politics and history.

The nature of premodern western power politics—and the politics in which the papacy engaged was no exception—can be difficult for us to understand today, especially in parts of the world where constitutionalism and the rule of law are prized as ideals. Even if these ideals are often unrealized (sometimes spectacularly so), they are at least goals at which society aims. Things were different in Machiavelli's time. The best way to explain the difference is to say that, for someone who had reached a position of prominence—as a leader in a city-state government, a member of a titled nobility, or as a high clerical leader—it would have been in bad taste not to help one's family and kin. Now, to say that nepotism was encouraged would be an exaggeration. Many of Machiavelli's predecessors in fifteenth-century Italy had made the argument that true virtue was located not in nobility or in a title but in the actions of an individual. Still, nepotism was much more accepted as a matter of course than it is today.

So when we see fifteenth-century Florentine thinkers, for example, reaching toward constitutional reform along republican lines, emphasizing protection of private property and other rights for individual citizens, what is clear is that their experience represents one important part of the long-range genealogy of modern constitutionalism. But Florentine government reform or Venetian republicanism, say, should not be confused with things like the U.S. Constitution. The world was fundamentally different then, and Machiavelli's gift was his ability to see that world as it was. And this gift was the result of inborn intelligence combined with on-the-ground experience during this crucial decade. At least two of Machiavelli's experiences are worth emphasizing: the time he spent in the orbit of Cesare Borgia and his involvement with the Florentine militia.

Since 1494 and the descent of the French, Italy's various city-states had been embroiled in conflict and intrigue, with ever-shifting alliances the norm and various leaders rising to prominence. One of these was Cesare Borgia, the son of Pope Alexander VI, whose intention it was to aggrandize the papal dominion, enrich his family, and strengthen the position of his kin. Machiavelli had the chance to observe Cesare Borgia closely. Borgia's rise was spectacular. Made a bishop at the age of fifteen and soon thereafter a cardinal, he renounced religious office to pursue the life of a *condottiere*, a military captain. Like many *condottieri*, Cesare Borgia had designs on Italian territory, designs that were consonant with those of his father, the pope. They made a perfect team, at least for a while.

Once Cesare resigned the office of cardinal (the first person ever to do so), the French king, Louis XII, with whom the Pope had allied, made Cesare the duke of Valentinois (covering more or less the region of Monaco). Duke Valentino, as Cesare was often known thereafter, commenced a series of military adventures, all with the backing of Pope Alexander. Alexander informed the rulers of a series of client states in Italy's Marches and Emilia-Romagna region (near Bologna) that he was cancelling their fiefs—meaning that he was annulling the agreement in place whereby they had sole authority over their states under the patronage of the pope. Needless to say, these leaders did not take the news well, and as Cesare gathered forces they met to decide on strategy.

As for Cesare and Alexander, their hope was to set up a large state in northeastern Italy, with Cesare at the head. At first

Cesare had Swiss troops sent by the king of France, and with them at his service he successfully conquered Imola and Forlì, key towns relatively close to Bologna. Then in 1500 Pope Alexander created twelve new cardinals. Like those appointed to prominent ambassadorial posts today by the U.S. president, cardinals then were often named because of the financial support they could offer the pope. The revenues provided by these new cardinals afforded Pope Alexander the ability to hire a series of *condottieri* along with their associated small armies, so that they could work together with Cesare. These hard-bitten men conquered a number of cities in the Romagna and the Marches. Meanwhile, his rapacity increasing, Cesare took to the south with the aid of French forces and ousted the leaders of Naples and Capua. Then Cesare headed back north to the Marches, capturing Urbino and Camerino. It was now clear that his ambitions outstripped his original aims, so much so that some of his hired *condottieri* began to suspect that they too would become his targets.

Machiavelli was present at Cesare Borgia's traveling court for parts of the years 1502 and 1503 and was an eyewitness to some of the events that gained Cesare his reputation for bloodthirstiness. Machiavelli's almost daily reports from that time, called "legations," show that Cesare Borgia, "Duke Valentino," represented an object of utter fascination for the young diplomat, one of the reasons why he would later dedicate a chapter of *The Prince* to Cesare's explosive career. In October 1502, Machiavelli writes to the Florentine government that Cesare Borgia is "spirited, fortunate, and full of hope, with the favor of both a pope and a king."[1] Then, a few months later, Machiavelli writes that one can see in Duke Valentino, "an almost unheard of fortune, and a super-human hope that he has the power to fulfill every one of his desires."[2] One observes Machiavelli's interest in larger-than-life figures, men who possess strength of personal character and happen to act at the right moment in history. Later, this interest would be overt in *The Prince* and in his other writings. At this early stage, it was nourished by direct observation.

The legations tell us much of what Machiavelli's life was like during these stress-filled but exhilarating years. Once, for example, when Cesare was looking for an overt alliance with Florence, we observe Machiavelli recognizing the limits of his own position as secretary. In the midst of tortured negotiations regarding a possible Florentine alliance, when the Borgia court found itself in the small city of Cesena, Machiavelli wrote to the Florentine Signoria and asked them to "send a man of high standing here rather than to Rome. The reason is that, with respect to the agreement that will need to be made, one will need to satisfy the man here [meaning Cesare Borgia], not the Pope." Any act of negotiation is best accomplished in one place, Machiavelli writes, "and it would be preferable to negotiate it here. . . . Given that I will not be and am not appropriate, since one would need someone with more discretion, more reputation, and someone who would understand more of the world than I do, I have always deemed it a good idea to send an Ambassador . . . everyone thinks as I do."[3]

"I am not appropriate." The word Machiavelli uses here, translated as "appropriate," is simply *buono*, which at its most literal level means "good." One might have translated it as "suitable" or "sufficient" as well. What the passage shows is that Machiavelli was well aware that he did not stem from the traditional families of the Florentine elite, whose members qualified to be sent as official ambassadors. As he refined his skills—his powers of observation, his political knowledge, and his increasingly incisive writing—he would come to believe that these were his most important tools, even as he could not help but recognize that, given his social standing, certain paths would always remain closed to him.

Cesare Borgia's grand plans came to an end soon after the death of his father, Pope Alexander, in 1503. After the very short reign of a pope favorable to Cesare (Pius III, who died after twenty-six days in office), Giuliano della Rovere was elected as Pope Julius II. He had military ambitions of his own, was a Borgia enemy, and with some careful plotting managed to seize the lands that Borgia held in the Papal States. Soon thereafter, Duke Valentino's emerging megastate crumbled into fragments, and once more Italy became a chessboard on which the strategies of the powerful would be enacted.

The first "literary" work that Machiavelli wrote—in *terza rima*, Dante's meter—was entitled the *Decennale*. As the title implies, the poem, written in 1504 (though not printed until 1506) was meant to give an account of the last *decennio*, or ten years. It told the story in other words of Florence from the moment when the French king, Charles VIII, made his momentous descent into Italy. Here is how Machiavelli summed up the fate of Borgia's fledgling state:

> *Poi che Alessandro fu dal ciel ucciso*
> *lo stato del suo duca di Valenz*
> *in molte parte fu rotto e diviso.*

[Then when Alexander was killed by the heavens
The state of his Duke of Valentino
Was broken and split into many parts.][4]

One year after these lines were published, the duke, betrayed by a supposed ally, was killed on the field of battle.

+   +   +

Machiavelli's experience with Cesare Borgia—his observation of Borgia's rise and fall and complicated military endeavors—led to the second experience that should be singled out in Machiavelli's career during that crucial first decade of the sixteenth century: his involvement with the Florentine militia. To understand its importance, one central fact needs to be brought into relief: war, or better, military campaigning, was a regular occurrence in Machiavelli's day.

Today we are accustomed to an idea that has its roots in the European Enlightenment of the eighteenth century, the idea of the possibility of perpetual peace. To arrive at a state of unending peace, it has also come to seem legitimate to throw everything one has into a war, to eliminate all possible enemies, notionally forever, with means as extreme as possible—to fight, in short, a "total" war in order to fight the "last" war. The massive, hitherto unheard of numbers of active fighters in World War I, the use of weapons of mass destruction in World War II, and even the Cold War nuclear policies of mutually assured destruction as a deterrent to further conflict all stem from this Enlightenment notion.[5] War could be ended forever by that one final war. As the late twentieth and early twenty-first centuries have shown in abundance, this principle sounds reasonable in theory but does not work in practice. Still, we do not today assume that every year will bring some sort of military campaign—and for those of us in the west who find ourselves tiring of what seem like constant military engagements, we should remember one thing: the real fighting is far from home.

Things were very different in Machiavelli's era. If one's city was besieged, it meant that hostile soldiers were literally at the door. And with late-medieval and Renaissance Italy's constant political machinations—with smaller states allying with larger ones, larger states allying with non-Italian powers, and conspiracies always in the air—the question was not whether a state would be engaged in military affairs, but how. Florence was no stranger to these matters. Like many other Italian states, the Florentine government employed *condottieri*, mercenary military captains not unlike Cesare Borgia. But Florence, especially by the early sixteenth century, had seen its share of failures. Especially problematic was the city of Pisa, which was important to Florence since it was so close to the sea and shared the Arno river, thus facilitating trade and commerce. In the *Decennale*, Machiavelli says that Florence suffered "four mortal wounds," three of which, the insurrections of the subject territories Pistoia, Arezzo, and Valdichiana, had been remedied, because Florence had found ways to quell them and retake control. The fourth, however, was Pisa, which had been in a state of rebellion. At the very end of the *Decennale*, Machiavelli's recommendation to the Florentines was that they "reopen the temple to Mars."[6] What Machiavelli meant became clear soon thereafter.

Machiavelli entered into a debate that had a history. To fight its wars, should a state hire paid, noncitizen soldiers, who had a loyalty to their military captain? Or would a state be stronger if its military force were drawn from among its own subjects? As to mercenaries, if the captain was reliable, one could be assured of both professional military expertise and loyalty to the state's objectives. But all too often, mercenaries and their captains had proven fickle allies, switching sides if better pay were offered or leaving when arduous conditions presented themselves. Florence suffered just such a humiliation when in the 1505 Pisan campaign the condottiere Giovanpaolo Baglioni left the field of battle.[7]

Citizen militias also presented advantages and disadvantages. They were in general more motivated, since they were fighting for their own city. Sustained by civic patriotism, they presumably fought longer and harder. Dante had fought for Florence at the Battle of Campaldino in 1289, and there were venerable examples from the ancient world, such as the philosopher Socrates fighting for Athens at Potidaea in 432 BC. Especially important for Machiavelli was the fact that his beloved ancient historian, Livy, presented the greatest victories of the ancient Roman Republic, in its early years, as the result of armies drawn from its subjects and citizens. Yet there were dangers as well, especially for the traditional ruling elites. An armed peasantry under the captaincy of a strong military ruler would naturally diminish the power of the elite families, and their fear was that Florence would become a princedom. In post-1502 Florence, these concerns were intensified by Piero Soderini's life tenure as *gonfaloniere*. Were he to have a small army at his beck and call, what would prevent him from becoming a prince, setting up a hereditary dynasty, and doing all the things that Florence's leading families had resisted for more than two centuries?

So when Machiavelli faced this problem, there was tension in the air. One final, and unexpected, particularity emerged. There was a rich tradition in medieval Italy of using symbols and ideas associated with ancient Rome.[8] And ever since the fascination for the ancient world had accelerated greatly in the fourteenth century, Florence like many other cities had become accustomed to holding public festivals with ancient Roman themes, recalling episodes from ancient Roman history in their civic culture, and even using ancient examples to help solve modern problems. Yet in the post-Savonarolan period, after 1498, there was resistance in Florence to using ancient Roman examples. Some opposition came from followers of Savonarola who, though their leader was dead, still resisted the use of secular ancient examples. Some opposition came about for other reasons, from a feeling that examples drawn from antiquity were irrelevant to modern life.

Machiavelli himself found this out in 1503 when he proposed a way to deal with a rebellious territory in the Florentine dominions, the Valdichiana (about thirty-five miles south of Florence, near the city of Arezzo). He wrote a recommendation in that year to the Signoria in which he was overt about his reasoning—too much so, as it turned out—relying heavily on a lengthy passage in Livy, which he translated verbatim and included in his short report.

The episode Machiavelli highlights took place in the year 338 BC, something important to note since that period formed part of the ancient Roman Republic's effort to consolidate its power and to bring nearby territories under its sway. Livy himself, who was writing his monumental *History of Rome from the City's Foundation* under the reign of Augustus (in the twenties BC), gave a somewhat idealized version of the early republic, as a time when small, disciplined Roman armies expanded Rome's reach and enlarged its dominion, aided by the virtue, severity, and seriousness of its leaders. In this respect, Livy was of a piece with Rome's most famous Augustan poet, Virgil, who memorably wrote that Rome's mission was "to impose the customs of peace, to vanquish the proud, and to give clemency to those who were its subjects."[9]

Machiavelli zeroes in on a speech to the Senate by Camillus, one of Rome's two consuls (its highest elected office then), who spoke at length about how to deal with rebellious territories in Rome's immediate environs. While there was obviously no recorded version, the speech, as Livy writes it, is presumed to reflect the intentions of the speaker and to give the gist of what he argued (the use of semifictional speeches was a commonplace in premodern history writing, Machiavelli's included). Camillus had just returned from a triumphant military expedition, in which he and his forces had violently put down a rebellion. Fueled by success, they went on to conquer all of Latium (today the larger province of Lazio, in which Rome is situated), which took its name from the "Latins," the designation of the people who lived there, referring both to the language they spoke and their kinship structure.

Camillus's speech suggests that the Senate may have been vacillating as to what to do with and to the conquered: "You have the ability to assure yourselves ever-lasting peace as far as concerns the Latins, something you may do exercising cruelty or forgiveness, at your discretion. Would you impose severe measures against those who have surrendered or been conquered? . . . Would you, following the example of your fathers, increase the Roman state by receiving the conquered as citizens?"[10] The classic Roman strategy, adopted repeatedly, was to adopt the conquered into the large and growing fabric of the Roman world, extending citizenship and many benefits in exchange for cooperation. The other option, as occurred later, during the Punic wars in 149 BC (something which Livy, writing retrospectively, may have had in mind), was to destroy the enemy utterly, leaving no possibility for revenge. Camillus goes on: "But now is the time for you to determine what you would like to do. You hold all those people in the palm of your hand, suspended between hope and fear. So two things are necessary. First, you must resolve your own concerns regarding them, and do so as soon as possible. Second, you must be clear with them whether you intend punishment or kindness, as they wait, stunned."[11] Camillus, in other words, having sized up the military situation, urges the Senate not to waver and instead to make a forthright decision and to follow it expeditiously.

It is worth expatiating on this long-ago episode in Roman history because Machiavelli himself used it at great length. Indeed, Machiavelli went so far as to cite Livy extensively, including almost all of Camillus's speech in his written recommendation to Florence's main governing body. Machiavelli argued that the Florentine government, vacillating as to what to do with the rebellious territory, should instead look toward the ancient Romans. His reasoning as to why is revealing: "I have heard it said that history is the teacher of our actions, especially when it comes to how to exercise rule. And the world has always been inhabited by men who share the same passions. There are those who serve and those who rule, and there are those who serve unwillingly and those who serve willingly. And there are those who rebel and who are retaken. If anyone doesn't believe this, take a look at Arezzo last year, and the Valdichiana, who are doing something quite similar to the Latins." Machiavelli means that in his view the current Tuscan situation is similar to that of Latium, as Livy has described it.[12]

So for Machiavelli the ancients mattered, and history was important as a guide, because there are fundamental continuities in human behavior and political balances of power. These things being the case, one should look toward ancient history when thinking about how to deal with the Valdichiana and one should "imitate those who were the masters of the world [the Romans], especially in a case where they teach you precisely how you should govern. . . . The Romans thought, once, that peoples who have rebelled should be given benefits [i.e., of citizenship] or exterminated, and that any other way was most dangerous."[13] Machiavelli goes on to say that neither has been done in the case of Arezzo. The Aretines, he says, as of now need to report regularly to Florence, their titles have been taken away, and their property has been sold. And Florence has not sent its own settlers to live there and to govern the town. The Aretines are, essentially, under occupation, being ruled remotely by Florence without sharing the benefits of rule.

"*Precisely* how you should govern" (*appunto* is the Italian word Machiavelli uses). Could an ancient example really teach one "precisely" what to do in the present? Perhaps it was this seeming overreliance on the validity of ancient Roman examples that led the Florentine government to reject Machiavelli's recommendation. One of Florence's many archival records preserves the response of one of the city's leaders, who summed up the consensus when Machiavelli's recommendation, to send settlers to Valdichiana and to give the citizens there "benefits," came up: "Sending new inhabitants there was something the Romans did, a custom not practiced at present. And to win them over with benefits cannot be done."[14] So Florence continued with what Machiavelli considered an ill-starred middle-way policy, occupying the city and thus humiliating the inhabitants, ruling remotely but ineffectively, and in general planting the seeds for further unrest. The failure of his plan in this instance taught him a lesson: practical politics needed to adapt to local circumstances.

When it came to reforming Florence's military affairs, Machiavelli was much more practical, realizing that there were obstacles in place and that, if he wanted his plan to succeed, he would have to navigate the shoals of recent history quite carefully. The Savonarolans, in the 1490s, had argued in favor of Florence developing its own militia, and back then the proposal had been defeated by Florentines who feared that what happened to Rome in the first century BC would happen to contemporary Florence: ambitious generals would rise and turn the city into a dictatorship. And since so many Italian states had in fact gone the way of a princedom, one worry on the part of Florence's ruling families was that Soderini, with his office of *gonfaloniere* for life, intended to become just such a ruler. So Machiavelli had to make sure he did not appear to be setting up Soderini as a prince in his *Rationale for Ordering the Militia*

(*Cagione dell'Ordinanza*), in which he addressed where to find the prospective soldiers and what needed to be done to train them. In contrast to his earlier written recommendation on the Valdichiana, this treatise contained no lofty references to ancient history, Livy, and so on, instead placing simple recommendations before Florentine leaders.

The treatise is not without Machiavelli's habitual bluntness (one might even call it a lack of tact). He does not speak in the language of the court, suggesting what one "might" do. Instead he avers that the only way for the city to re-arm itself is to establish this possibility through "public deliberation" and to sustain it in a well-ordered way. He goes on: "Don't worry about the hundred-some years that you have lived and otherwise sustained yourselves, since if you think carefully about those times and these, you will realize that it is impossible to preserve your liberty in the same way."[15] There is an implied critique, to the effect that the Florentines may have lapsed into a lack of vigilance. And there is that worst of things—from a traditional Florentine perspective—noted as a danger: the possible loss of liberty. This word, "liberty," has an important pedigree in the Florentines' own discussions about their forms of government. The term sometimes pointed to the desire for more broad-based representative forms of government. In Machiavelli's era, however, it tended to mean the "liberty" of the ruling class, freedom from princely control, and freedom from dependency on non-Florentine patrons. The city, notionally, should stand as an independent state with all the qualities this independence implied, most notably having other local territories under its sway. Machiavelli was suggesting that, to accomplish these ends, Florence needed to have its own military force. The question was where to find the requisite military recruits from among three possible areas. Should they come from the city itself? Should they be drawn from the surrounding *contado*—the rural areas of Florentine territory outside the city walls but close by? Or could one target the *distretto*, or "district," which was the formal designation for the areas further out that were still technically under Florentine dominion?

Machiavelli suggests that they must recruit from the *contado*. His reasoning is that there are always people who give orders and people who obey, and in armies there are those who fight on horseback and those who are infantry. Since the city of Florence itself is full of people who have horses and the associated dignities, including the propensity to give orders, and since the *distretto* is too unstable, the real need is to look to the *contado*. There one could find a willing peasantry whose members would be willing to serve as infantry.

Machiavelli reveals a tendency that runs through all of his work: the propensity to observe human beings and their behavior like an anthropologist *avant la lettre*. He is much less concerned with observing what should be the case. He concentrates rather on what is the case. Here this inclination emerges as he suggests how one should create the proper symbols and habitual behaviors for the soldiers. To have the military plan work correctly, one would need flags and symbols that should be associated with the leaders under whom they are to fight, "so that all your men become emotionally committed to one and the same thing."[16] The recruits should be paid for their service. There should be periodic festivals and parades, and the leadership should, "on certain days and certain times . . . mix in a little bit of religion to make them more compliant."[17] There should be a separate magistracy created in Florence that administers the military in time of peace (whereas in wartime The Ten, the magistracy, composed of ten men, that traditionally dealt with these matters, would take over administration). The appointed constables should be changed each year. Should the plan to organize the military in the *contado* succeed, that example would then radiate back into the city. Military service would become a point of patriotic pride. Machiavelli went on to give quite practical suggestions, a set of bylaws really, that set out the details of governance, the various titles needed (the new magistracy that would supervise the militia in peacetime was to be called "The Nine"), stipends, punishments for infractions, and types of foot soldiers.

Machiavelli avoided drawing overtly on any ancient examples from Livy, even if it seems clear (as we can see from later writings) that the ancient Roman republican example—filtered through Livy as read by Machiavelli—was uppermost in his mind. Later, in his profound work of historical commentary, his *Discourses on the First Decade of Livy*, Machiavelli wrote, by way of introducing a lengthy citation from Livy, "with Livy's testimony anyone may understand how a good militia is formed."[18] But it was too hot a topic in the Florence of his day, and Machiavelli cared too much about having his plan work out in practice, to weigh it down with too much theory. And work it did.

Having persuaded Soderini to allow him to begin, Machiavelli went to one of the *contado* areas and began recruiting. By 1506 he had a group of four hundred newly recruited *fanti*, or infantry, come to Florence for a military display. A contemporary chronicler captured the mood: "thus there was held the most beautiful thing that was ever put together for the city of Florence."[19] Machiavelli persuaded the Signoria to hire don Michelotto, who had been Cesare Borgia's brutal paid assassin and henchman, to be one of the military leaders, over the objections of those who feared that Machiavelli was trying to set Soderini up as a prince. And finally, Machiavelli's hoped-for new magistracy was created, "The Nine," who were charged with supervising the militia in times of peace. He was made its head, a position he held until 1512, along with his two other offices. Though the anticipated 10,000 troops proved too high a number to recruit, eventually Machiavelli was able to reach 5,000. This impressive feat was not lost on contemporaries, as another observer stressed that Machiavelli's military was gaining such a reputation "that all of Italy was watching, and especially the republic of Venice."[20]

As Florentine forces engaged in military maneuvers to retake Pisa, Machiavelli was there, ordering provisions, regulating their conduct, and keeping up his profuse correspondence with his Florentine superiors. He worked on plans with engineers to divert the river Arno in an attempt to deprive Pisa of access.[21] One of the infantry battalions had reached such a point that he could proudly write, in 1509, that he believed it was the finest in Italy.[22] Ultimately, while his infantry did not fight any major battles, their organization allowed Florence to achieve its objective, which was to shut off Pisa's contact with the outside world. They did so effectively enough that in 1509 Pisa formally surrendered. Machiavelli was among those who signed the surrender agreement on the part of the victors, and his colleagues and superiors recognized him as having played a major part in the triumph over Pisa, as having closed the "fourth wound."

One colleague wrote him to say that the news had reached Florence: "everyone is going crazy with happiness. There are bonfires all over the city."[23] Machiavelli had reached the apex of his public career.

Machiavelli's personal triumph, however, did not mean that the government of Piero Soderini was out of danger. Since 1494, when the Medici fell, there had been three elements in the mix when it came to the difficult question of how Florence should be governed. There were the Medici, for one thing, always waiting in the wings even when out of power, with a powerful member of the family, Giovanni de' Medici, installed as a cardinal in Rome (he would become Pope Leo X in 1513). The son of Lorenzo the Magnificent, Giovanni lived lavishly, cultivating friends and allies in Rome and even back in Florence, as he married off his niece to a member of the Strozzi family, one of Florence's most prominent and powerful clans.

And then there developed, hazily at the time but clearer in retrospect, two different varieties of "republicanism," one narrow, the other broad. *Ottimati* was the term used to designate members of Florentine families who were recognized by contemporaries as occupying the highest echelons of Florentine society. They were the kind of people deemed worthy to serve as ambassadors (as Machiavelli was not). Names included the Medici of course, along with the Strozzi, the Rucellai, the Salviati, and others. Anti-Medicean *ottimati* had hoped, after the ouster of Piero de' Medici in Florence, to set up a republic modeled on Venice: aristocratic, with governance reserved to a closed number of families. The Savonarolan adventure of 1494–1498, however, had opened the way to a broader notion, as certain governing institutions expanded to include participation by citizens of different classes. In the sources of the time, they are called the *popolo*, the "people," though one would not want to make the mistake of thinking of this as anything like a modern democracy. (The *popolo* often included merchants and others who had made a fair amount of money and done so recently, so that their families did not qualify as *ottimati* in the social memory of Florentine elites.) The *ottimati* remained horrified at the passions unleashed during the Savonarolan period, hoping that the government of Soderini would allow the institution of a Venetian republican type of system. But Soderini, though never a Savonarolan, had different constituencies to placate, occasionally making gestures to the *popolo* and involving more people in activities of governance.

By 1512 these forces of instability brought about a change of government, and the balance tipped back in favor of the Medici. In the interim between his military triumph and 1512, Machiavelli was sent on missions to France, Siena, and to the court of Monaco. Florence remained tenuously allied with France. The result was that, when Pope Julius II, Venice, the duke of Ferrara, and Ferdinand the Catholic of Spain formed a "Holy League" against French interests and decided in 1512 to work to restore the Medici to Florence, trouble was inevitable for the Soderini government. By August 31, 1512, after the Spanish had sacked Florence's nearby subject city, Prato, Soderini was compelled to abdicate, fleeing to what is now southern Croatia.

Thereafter things happened quickly in Florence, as the Medici and their allies effected what was termed a *mutatione*— or "change"—of government. Machiavelli, in a contemporary letter (possibly written to Isabella d'Este, marquess of Mantua, mentioned with affection in Baldassare Castiglione's

Courtier, and a well known patron of culture) recounted the events after Medici partisans seized the Palazzo della Signoria and Florence was thrown into chaos: "the whole city was up in arms, and that name [*the Medici*] resonated throughout the city. The result was that the Signoria was compelled to call the people to an assembly, which we call a *parlamento.* There a law was promulgated that reinstalled these magnificent Medici, with all the honors and rank of their ancestors." The next sentence is revelatory: "And the city is very peaceful and hopes with their help to carry on with no less honor than it did in the past, when their father Lorenzo, of such happy memory, governed."[24] Though Soderini was now gone, Machiavelli hoped to continue to serve the government of Florence.

He wrote a short recommendation to the Medici then in power in November 1512, arguing that they should help restore the old republican regime, what Machiavelli calls the "old order" or *ordine vecchio.* Machiavelli further cautioned the Medici that they should fear the rise of those who "do not want to help this State, but rather increase their own reputation." In other words, Machiavelli warned of the dangers of an aristocratic regime, suggesting that the Medici should return to an older, pre-Savonarolan republicanism. The emotion and repetitiveness of this short treatise indicate someone in a turbulent frame of mind who, justifiably as it turned out, feared for his future.[25]

During that same month of November 1512, the new, pro-Medici Signoria removed Machiavelli from his offices, sentencing him to remain in Florentine territories for a year. Soon thereafter a list emerged that two anti-Medici Florentines had prepared as they were planning a conspiracy against the Medici and their supporters. The list contained names of people whom they hoped to involve in the conspiracy. One of those names was Machiavelli's. On February 19, 1513, a town crier made an announcement on behalf of the Florentine committee charged with police matters (The Eight) to this effect: anyone of any rank who knew of the whereabouts of "Niccolò di Bernardo Machiavegli [i.e., Machiavelli] must, within an hour of the time of this announcement, have made this known to the said Eight under penalty of being considered a rebel and of having their property confiscated."[26] And, though there is no evidence that Machiavelli supported the conspiracy, he was taken, jailed, and subjected to torture. From contemporary correspondence, we learn that the vehicle of torture was the *strappado*, where one's hands are tied behind the back, one is raised by rope to the ceiling and then dropped, with the rope held just before one hits the ground so that the arms are jerked up, sometimes out of their sockets. Machiavelli's imprisonment lasted twenty-two days, his release occurring after the election of Le Giovanni de' Medici as Pope Leo X on March 11, 1513.

Machiavelli's close friend Francesco Vettori, a Florentine Ambassador to Rome, helped in freeing Machiavelli, as we learn from a letter exchange between them. Machiavelli's desire to be back in the theater of politics is touchingly apparent at the close of his letter to Vettori (13 March): "Keep me in the front of His Lordship's mind, if you can, so that if at all possible he, or his people, might start to engage my services for anything suitable, since I believe I would do something honorable for you, and useful for me." Even then, even after imprisonment and torture, the Secretary wanted one thing most of all: to be back in the game. Vettori responds: "I have had no greater sorrow than when I learned you had been imprisoned, since I knew right away that without crime or cause you would suffer torture, as indeed occurred. How it grieves me not to have been able to help you . . . I did so however when the pope was elected, and I asked for nothing else than your liberation."[27]

Machiavelli's letters reveal the nature of the world in which he lived: no *habeas corpus*, no sense of individual human rights, no guarantees. Personal connections mattered most in staying safe and finding work. Machiavelli's correspondence from this period also reveals that Vettori was trying to help him, attempting to win permission for Machiavelli to leave Florence. And Machiavelli's letters evince the same desire to go to work, either in Florence or in Rome at the papal court. Machiavelli believes he is qualified for only one thing: "since Fortune has seen to it that—because I don't know how to talk about the trade in silk or wool, nor of profits and losses—I need to talk about politics."[28]

And indeed, a reader can feel Machiavelli reviving palpably in these letters when he comes to the discussion of political affairs. In these months, the stimulus for these reflections comes when Vettori asks Machiavelli for political opinions and Machiavelli has the chance to develop longer arguments about the politics of the French and the Spanish. His tone breathes confidence, the thinking is more structured, and the letters less full of self-pity. Typical in this regard is a letter to Vettori from August 26, 1513, where in reply to Vettori's summary of politics Machiavelli writes: "As far as the state of things in this world goes, here is the conclusion I draw from them: we are governed by princes who, by nature or by chance, possess the following qualities. We have a smart pope, who because of this quality is both serious and careful; an emperor who is unstable and fickle; a king of France who is disdainful and fearful; a king of Spain both miserly and greedy; a king of England who is rich, ferocious, and desirous of glory; and the Swiss, who are like animals, accustomed to victory and insolent." The rest of the letter presents Machiavelli's reasoning for precisely why these things are the case and ends with the fear that Italy will fall into "servitude that, if it does not occur today or tomorrow, will occur in our lifetime."[29]

Servitude. How to avoid it? Machiavelli's fear here was as much for Italy as for himself.

3

Interlude

✦   ✦   ✦

Clues concerning Machiavelli's thinking as to his own immediate personal path lie in one of the Italian Renaissance's most
beautiful—and in some ways most deceiving—letters, which
he wrote to his friend Vettori on December 10, 1513.[1] There had
been a brief interruption in their correspondence, one that left
Machiavelli concerned. But upon receiving Vettori's latest letter
Machiavelli is "most pleased," he says, and since he has no news
to report resolves to send Vettori an account of what his life in
exile is like. "I am on my farm, and I haven't been in Florence
for more than twenty days, total, since my recent problems."
Machiavelli spent about a month hunting thrushes—"two
at least, at most six"—each day. After this diversion ended,
Machiavelli settled into a routine: "In the mornings I rise with
the sun, and I go to one of my woods that I am having cleared,
where I stay for two hours to look over the work done the day
before and to spend some time with the woodsmen. They are
always in the middle of some argument, either among themselves or with the neighbors." Machiavelli mixes and mingles

with people of all classes, even as he listens to and participates in arguments. This fact was probably unsurprising to Vettori, knowing his friend as he did, even as it might seem surprising to connoisseurs of "high" literature.

"After I leave the woods, I go to a spring, and thereafter to a place where I hang my bird nets. I have a book with me— Dante, or Petrarch, or a minor poet, like Tibullus, Ovid, or other ones of that sort. I read about their romantic passions, their love affairs, and I remember my own, taking pleasure for a while in those thoughts." From the social to the solitary: this seems to be the second phase of his day, where repeated reading of a light classic, something that he already has read many times but to which he willingly returns, allows him to reflect on his own life. After this diversion and care of the soul comes more interactivity: "Then I take to the road, on the way to the inn. I chat with people who pass by, ask them about the news where they live, learning this and that, and I take note of the diverse taste and imaginings of men." Machiavelli's curiosity and, again, his proto-anthropological sensibility, is on display here.

A meal follows—"whatever there is to eat that this poor farm and my tiny means afford me"—and then he returns to the inn, where he finds "the innkeeper, normally, a butcher, a miller, and a couple of kiln-workers. I bum around with them for the rest of the day," playing cards and backgammon and, again, arguing: "these games lead to a thousand disagreements and endless insults." We sense a Machiavelli at home in different environments, who needs the give and take of vigorous human interaction.

There then follows the letter's best known part, Machiavelli's account of the conclusion of his day:

Once the evening has arrived, I come home and enter my study. In the entryway I take off my daytime clothing, covered with mud and dirt, and I put on garments that are royal, and suitable for a court. Changed into suitable clothes, I step into the ancient courts of ancient men. Received lovingly by them, I nourish myself on that food that alone is mine, for which I was born. There I am unashamed to talk with them and ask them the reasons for their actions, and they, with their humanity, answer me. For four hours I feel no boredom, I forget all worries, I do not fear poverty, and am not dismayed by death. I give myself to them entirely.

Every line of this description is important. Machiavelli tells us he enters his "study"—his *scrittoio*—which, for those people who wrote and read in the Renaissance, was a kind of sacred space, where you received your most intimate friends in a space adorned with the books, art, and objects that meant the most to you. These Renaissance studies represented a place of private contemplation in a world where privacy was not easy to find. So Machiavelli's deliberate foregrounding of his study tells Vettori—and his readers—that what he does there takes on a particular, and personal, importance.

Furthermore, though as we shall see Machiavelli makes no absolute statements in any of his works as to the best form of government—that is, whether a republic or monarchy is best, and so on—here, in the realm of literature and history, among his beloved ancients, he is among royalty and, he says, he must dress the part: "I put on garments that are royal, and suitable for a court," so that he can "step into the ancient courts of ancient men." The ancients receive him "lovingly," and Machiavelli says: "I nourish myself on that food that alone is mine, for which I was born." The expression translated here as "nourish myself"—*mi pasco*—can be translated more literally in Italian as "I graze." Machiavelli is suggesting, in other words, that for him reading the ancients is something purely and totally natural—"the food for which I was born." Then, "I am unashamed to talk with them." This is a realm where there are none of the hierarchies of wealth and privilege that, in the real workaday world of politics, inevitably manifest themselves.

When he asks the ancients the reasons for their actions, "they, with their humanity, answer me." This word, "humanity," sends another important signal. The Italian word—*umanità*—recalls the Latin in which Machiavelli was practically bathed as a young student and specifically the word *humanitas*, which in its ancient resonances (which Machiavelli well knew) signified more than an attribute distinguishing a human being from an animal. As Aulus Gellius (an ancient author much loved in the Renaissance) put it, "humanity" meant "something like what the Greeks call *paideia*, and what we mean when we speak of education and initiation into the liberal arts. . . . Cultivation and learning in this type of knowledge has been given to man alone from among all animate beings and is therefore called 'humanity.'"[2] Learning, and specifically learning in the liberal arts, gave one the quality of *humanitas*, and for Machiavelli it is this precise quality that the ancient authors he loves so well possess.

Then there emerges the letter's most tantalizing moment, one that is again worthy of extended citation:

Because Dante says that one does not possess knowledge without retaining what one has understood, I
have jotted down what I have profited from in their
conversation, and I have composed a short work *De
principatibus*, where, in so far as I can, I delve in and
do some thinking about this subject, discoursing on
what a princedom is, what sorts of princedoms there
are, how they are acquired, how they are maintained,
and why they are lost. And if ever any of my musings
have pleased you, this one, I think, will not incur your
displeasure. And it should be received by a prince and
especially by a new prince; but I dedicate it to the Magnificence of Giuliano [de' Medici]. Filippo Casavecchia
has seen it, and he can inform you, at least in part,
about the thing itself and about the thoughts I have
shared about it with him, even as I continually enlarge
and polish it.

Machiavelli begins the paragraph with a Dantean commonplace, one that would be familiar to Vettori, drawn from Dante's
Paradiso, the third book of the *Divine Comedy* (following the
Inferno and the *Purgatorio*). There Dante's beloved Beatrice is
speaking to him, explaining to Dante what vows mean: "Open
your mind to what I am clarifying for you, and fix it in your
memory, since one does not possess knowledge without retaining what one has understood."[3] While Beatrice urges Dante
to fix in his memory what she is saying, Machiavelli indicates
that he has written down his thoughts *On Princedoms*, using
the Latin *De principatibus*, instead of Tuscan. And he gives

Vettori a taste of what the treatise is like, but only a taste, mentioning a few things he will treat there.

Machiavelli manifests a modest confidence in his work ("if ever any of my musings have pleased you"), and he also shows that he is still, though in the country, hoping to come back into the city, into the theater of politics. Between the time that this letter was written and the final composition of *The Prince*—for this is the treatise he is talking about—the dedicatee would change. But like many figures in the Renaissance, Machiavelli understood that, to succeed, he would need a patron, and he was using all his cunning to figure out to whom he might dedicate this work. He also indicates that he has shared his work with a friend and ally close to home, Filippo Casavecchia, also known to Vettori.

One more aspect comes into relief, something that tells us why this famous letter can be deceiving to modern ears. The contents summary Machiavelli gives here ("what a princedom is," and so on) covers more or less the contents of the first eleven of the twenty-six chapters in *The Prince*. And at the end Machiavelli says that he is continually "enlarging and polishing" his work. These comments have attracted scholars' attention, since they can help in studying the history of the composition of *The Prince*, a worthy goal (some have suggested, for example, that *The Prince* was composed in two distinct phases, with this letter marking the completion of phase one). But they are also important for another reason.

The most striking passage of this letter occurs when Machiavelli tells of that phase of the day, the evening, when he enters his study, changing his clothes to enter into "conversation," as he terms it, with the ancients. The picture drawn is of a solitary intellectual, who, though he might earlier in the day have joked and debated with others, was totally alone when it came to the reading and writing that led to *The Prince* and his other works. And it is certainly true that for much of the time he was indeed alone, away from the city that he loved, and secluded in his study. It is an appealing image, one that could almost come out of the nineteenth century, when a Romantic, brooding author would, notionally, toil alone and present his finished work to the world when he had completed it to his satisfaction. But this famous passage should be read together with the last passage cited, in which Machiavelli mentions both sharing his work with a friend and the fact that he is continually working on it.

Despite all the work Machiavelli did alone, the way authorship and "publishing" worked was different then. Machiavelli's creative process was more social than the romantic image implies. The goal was not to publish widely in the way we understand that term today, where one can imagine a unitary work, finished, with the possibility of publishing thousands of exactly identical copies, if not more. Printing with moveable type then was still new enough that it functioned in people's imaginations as a kind of accelerated way of producing manuscripts (hand-written texts). Also, because printing was an art that still operated by hand (rather than with the steam-powered presses of the early nineteenth century), one simply could not imagine, in the way an aspiring author can do today, what it might mean to have massive numbers of copies circulating worldwide. *The Prince*, in fact, was never printed during Machiavelli's lifetime, even though he would have had every chance to do so. He had print-published his first *Decennale* in 1506, so we know he was familiar with what it took to get things published in print.

But for Machiavelli, "publishing" meant "making public," and it meant doing so to his most important audience: those whom he considered close enough friends and intellectual colleagues that they could both engage in intelligent discussion with him about what he wrote and who, also, could help his work find the audience he desired through their networks. In this case, Machiavelli sincerely hoped that *The Prince* would help him find a job with the new Florentine regime or, if not there, then in Rome at the papal court, now that a Florentine was pope. In other cases, his imagined audience was different, as were his aims in writing. Yet in almost all instances the local environment played an important part. Machiavelli was not a Romantic author thinking universal thoughts in systematic ways, nor was he a political science professor propounding a unified political theory. Deeply sensitive to history and to the way fortune inflected human decisions, Machiavelli was a thinker whose most profound insights came when he documented and commented on change and instability. There is no better work in which to see these tendencies than in his undisputed masterpiece, *The Prince*.

4

The Prince

• • •

Few works command such fascination as Machiavelli's *The Prince*. By the end of the sixteenth century, it had been translated into numerous languages, placed on the Index of Prohibited Books (the Catholic Church's list of books that were forbidden owing to their perceived immorality), and become—as had Machiavelli himself—a symbol into which many meanings could be read: for Protestants an emblem of unethical Catholic Italy, for Catholics a symbol of Protestants' negative break from tradition, and even, for one of the theorists of the scientific revolution, Francis Bacon, an admired predecessor. Bacon wrote (a bit later, in 1605) that "we are much beholden to Machiavelli and others, that write what men do, and not what they ought to do."[1] The influence of *The Prince* has made it a focal point for scholars, who have sought to see how it has affected the modern world. It has also turned Machiavelli into a reference point for modern businesses, made "Machiavellian" an adjective in common use to refer to someone without fixed moral scruples, and made Machiavelli one of the (admittedly many) hinges around which popular culture turns.

Despite all the scholarship and popular culture that have had Machiavelli at their center, *The Prince* holds surprises and can open doors that we may not have known were there. The most powerful vantage point from which to consider the book is through the lens of what we can term "Machiavelli as observer." Every one of his most important insights emerges from his close observation of human behavior, whether it was conduct that he immediately witnessed or behavior he studied in the ancient texts he loved so well. Machiavelli saw it this way himself, as we can see from his Preface dedicated to the younger Lorenzo de' Medici (the grandson of Lorenzo the Magnificent, and one who Machiavelli presumed might be involved in running Florence). There, Machiavelli says that many people, to win the favor of a prince, give elaborate gifts. He instead has only one thing to offer: "knowledge of the actions of great men, which I have learned by long experience in modern affairs and a continuous study of ancient matters, which I have thought through with great effort and subjected to scrutiny."[2]

Machiavelli's reading, writing, and life experience were seamlessly connected for him, and they were guided by another fundamental conviction: that human emotions have always been the same, as he writes in the *Discourses*: "Everything that occurs in the world, in every epoch, has something that corresponds to it in ancient times. The reason is that these things were done by men ["human beings," obviously], who have and have always had the same passions."[3] We shall return to the *Discourses*, which are so evocative of the way Machiavelli composed, in Chapter 5. But for now it suffices to highlight Machiavelli's basic, bedrock assumption: the study of history should be combined with analysis of current events. This combination constituted the basic set of building blocks for how one should discuss political questions, given that human beings share a fundamental sameness, in their emotions at least, across time and culture.

Delving into *The Prince*, we find things that remind us of ourselves, precisely because, in one respect at least, Machiavelli was right. However much technology and industry have changed our lives, human behavior, emotions, and relationships share many similarities over time. We were then and still are human beings. This is why *The Prince* is all the more remarkable: although we find ourselves in it, when we look at the circumstances of its composition—from the language in which Machiavelli wrote it to the techniques with which he did so—we find ourselves in a different world entirely.

First, there is the language of *The Prince*, its beautiful, lapidary, often funny and homespun, but utterly elegant Tuscan. Machiavelli owed that language, in a direct and traceable way, to the previous century's struggles to find a language suitable for works of literature and philosophy, a language that needed two qualities. First, it had to match in seriousness and durability the power of Latin. Second, this new language needed to be flexible and modern enough to express contemporary realities. Machiavelli came of age precisely when Italian thinkers had, if sometimes only implicitly, answered those questions. Through careful research and debate, fifteenth-century Italian thinkers had discovered that ancient Latin had once been a living natural language. By the time Machiavelli was coming to maturity many Italian thinkers could write Latin not only fluently, a trait common to all intellectuals in the Middle Ages and Renaissance, but also expressively, flexibly, and in line with classical models. But the question was now becoming, not *could* they write in Latin, but *should* they write in Latin? Having studied Latin so well and by that study having increased their knowledge of grammar and linguistic structure, could they now take the next momentous step and write serious and important literature and history in Italian?

Ultimately the answer was yes. Machiavelli became part of a first, somewhat revolutionary generation of writers that included Castiglione (the author of *The Courtier*, a guide to education and manners for Italy's, and eventually Europe's elites) and even, by the end of the sixteenth century, Galileo. Latin was still the language that enabled authors to communicate across Europe's intelligentsia much more efficiently than any vernacular. But for Machiavelli and others like him, Italian, and specifically Tuscan, became the standard. Yet it was Tuscan in a certain mode: classicizing and formal, it was a language whose new, groundbreaking users had learned and absorbed the lessons of permanence that intense fifteenth-century study of Latin had provided. As early as 1473, one professor in the University of Florence put it this way, when he gave an opening oration to a course he was to teach on the fourteenth-century luminary Petrarch: "whoever wants to be a good Tuscan must be a good Latin first."[4] What he meant was that anyone who wanted both to understand and, importantly, to write Tuscan in an elevated and literary way needed to have thorough command of the rules and structure of Latin. Machiavelli was certainly a member of that restricted elite.

It often surprises modern readers that all of the twenty-six chapter titles in *The Prince* are in Latin and that Machiavelli dots his writing with Latin quotations and phrases. Many times translations simply elide these things, justifiably rendering all of the text into the target language. But for Machiavelli—and the people he hoped would read and discuss his work—the use of Latin, even in such a seemingly minor matter as chapter titles, served an important function. It reminded readers that what was on the page had aspirations to permanence. It suggested that the author was someone who was learned in precisely the way he claimed, well versed in ancient history, itself written in Latin and read in the original language. And finally, it served as a cue to "insiders," as if to say, "if you understand these Latinisms, you too can share in this inner circle of learning."

Another fact that can surprise modern readers is something we have already noted: that Machiavelli did not work hard to have *The Prince* printed during his lifetime and that it remained unprinted at the time of his death. So for whom was Machiavelli writing? An answer to that question can be gleaned from the structure of *The Prince* itself, something that, yet again, takes us not into the modern world (as so often happens with Machiavelli), but instead back into the fifteenth-century background out of which Machiavelli emerged. The structure of *The Prince* evokes a real-life counterpart to the many Latin dialogues that were written during the fifteenth century: learned discussions among presumed social equals of scholarly topics and the way they impacted contemporary life. These conversations occurred in small social groups—the secretaries and other high-ranking personnel at the papal court, for example, were famous for their learned, and sometimes lewd, discussions—and were memorialized in a literary form quite prized in the fifteenth century: the dialogue.

Thinkers wrote on topics of concern, as did Poggio Bracciolini, a secretary at the papal court, chancellor of Florence, and one of Florence's official historians (a function Machiavelli

himself would later fill). One of Poggio's dialogues was entitled *On Avarice*.[5] In it, his interlocutors explored what function was served by what we would now call the acquisition of
capital. Was it something to be denounced as a sin? Or, done
well, was it to be celebrated, as something that could encourage
virtue, since a wealthy person could do good things with his
money? Another thinker, the less known Lapo da Castiglionchio the Younger, wrote a dialogue called *On the Benefits of the
Papal Court*.[6] His interlocutors in that dialogue lay out the
many "benefits" one can gain from working at the papal court.
But as they enumerate how well many prelates live—with lavish
banquets and even prostitution detailed as "benefits"—one realizes that the dialogue could easily be read as satirical. What
is important, however, about both of these examples (which together represent only a small drop in the sea of fifteenth-century
dialogues) is that they practically demand a response. The
reader of a dialogue becomes, in a sense, another interlocutor,
able, and by the very literary form, encouraged to think of his
or her own responses. The point is that as a genre of writing,
the dialogue is conversational.

So too are letters, as we have seen looking at some of Machiavelli's own correspondence. The letter-writer expected a
response, even as he or she was responding to a previous letter.
Truth was to be worked out in a conversational way, shaped
by interaction with others. Fifteenth-century thinkers prized
this genre of writing as well, and Machiavelli himself was a
master letter-writer.

So how does all of this relate to *The Prince?* Its chapters are
all relatively short, first of all, comparable in size to letters. And
the tone of *The Prince* is conversational—while it is not formally

a dialogue, it has that same spirit, since Machiavelli often addresses the prospective "prince" for whom the work is written as "you" and speaks himself in the vivacious first person throughout. "Having recounted here all the actions of the duke [Valentino—i.e., Cesare Borgia], I wouldn't know how to fault him," says Machiavelli after telling the story of Cesare Borgia.[7] Machiavelli recounts the difficulties of a "new" princedom, in other words what can happen if a prince takes over another place with different languages and customs. One remedy is to go live there, as the Turks did in Greece (after the fall of Constantinople in 1453). "Being there, you can see problems arise as they are coming to be and nip them in the bud."[8]

"You" and "I": Machiavelli is writing as if he is having a conversation, as if he expects the reader to interact with him. Returning to the question of why this treatise remained unprinted in his lifetime, we can see what "publication" might have meant for Machiavelli. There was a target audience to whom he was speaking, a relatively restricted number of suitable listeners and readers who, he hoped, could prepare the way for him to reenter political life. Machiavelli's conversation—which we witness on the page in *The Prince*—was something he hoped would jump off the page and become a reality by being taken up in the right circles. He was not proposing a work of "political theory" notionally valid for all time, to be permanently memorialized in print. Instead, here, as often in his work, he was engaging in a conversation, "publishing" his voice and opinions to those who mattered.

The Prince can be viewed from many standpoints, and readers have labored long and hard to figure out its structure. But the first thing to note is its general tone, something that Machiavelli himself describes to his dedicatee right at the beginning. "I have not made this work excessively ornate, nor have I filled it up with fancy clauses and pompous, magniloquent words, nor with any other artifice or ornament that would be extrinsic to its purpose."[9] Others might do this sort of thing when they write to princes, but not Machiavelli. By contrast, "I don't want it to be considered presumptuous if a man of low and meager estate dares to examine and provide a framework for the way princes are to govern. Just as those who depict landscapes place themselves low on the plain when considering the nature of mountains and high places, and, when they consider low-lying locations place themselves high up, on top of the mountains, just so, in order to know the nature of the people one must be a prince and in order to know well the nature of princes it is useful to be a man of the people."[10]

So, the tone: Machiavelli wants to write clearly, simply, and effectively. On the one hand he is humbly aware of his own non-princely status. On the other, he asserts his "right to write," as it were, acknowledging with his painterly metaphor that different perspectives are necessary to observe things correctly, that one must stand back from one's own status and viewpoint in order to depict matters most effectively.

At the most general level, *The Prince* is divided into twenty-six short chapters. The first eleven comprise a unit and were likely what Machiavelli had in mind when he wrote to his friend Vettori to say that he was working on "a little book on princedoms." This part takes up a little more than 40 percent of the overall text and presents a loose typology of princedoms or, as the title to chapter one presents it: "What are the different types of princedoms, and how they are acquired." Readers learn over the next ten chapters what the different types of princedoms are, in Machiavelli's view, and what are the specific challenges that come with each type. The remaining chapters offer observations and advice on how to be a prince—how to comport oneself, how to preserve one's reputation, how to behave in different political contexts. Running through the book are four linked concerns, to which Machiavelli returns repeatedly: the need, when discussing politics, to look through the lens of the world as it is (rather than how it should be if we could re-imagine it according to our own abstract principles), the power of individuals (of their personalities and of their choices) in shaping events, the exercise of power, and finally—and always—the presence of instability in the world.

The first of these concerns (looking at the world as it is, not as it ought to be) emerges in almost every chapter. But Machiavelli does at times highlight this underlying interest, nowhere more so than in chapter fifteen, titled "Concerning those things for which men, and especially princes, are praised or blamed." Ostensibly the chapter—and much of the rest of the book at this point, Machiavelli intimates—has to do with the different things a prince needs to do to be effective: personal habits, virtues, techniques, and so on.

Machiavelli realizes that he is doing something different: "I recognize that many have written about these matters. It is on this account that I am concerned not to seem presumptuous, especially insofar as I have departed substantially from what others have suggested in discussing these matters."[11] Machiavelli well understands that, from antiquity onward, there was an almost unbroken tradition of political writing that concerned how an ideal community should be structured, what form of political life is best, and how to lead. Far from the academic habit of doing a "literature review," which in Machiavelli's day, like ours, would have consisted of surveying relevant writings that preceded his own, Machiavelli seems well aware of his novelty. The reason? "My intention is to write something useful to the person who receives it, so it has seemed more appropriate to me to go straight to the concrete truth of the matter, rather than what might be imagined about it."[12] He cannot stop there with his blanket criticism of what has preceded him: the truth is that "many have imagined republics and princedoms that have never been seen or known to exist in reality."[13] Again Machiavelli had in mind an audience—one that it is helpful for us to keep in mind as well, tempted as we might be to fit him into a school of thought in political theory. He was addressing himself to people who wanted and needed nothing more than an analysis of how to rule based on concrete examples and stripped of all idealism, the kind of people who might admire his bold and unusual stroke and help him get back into political life in some fashion.

Immediately thereafter, Machiavelli suggests the real reason why what he calls "imagination" has played such a large part, too large, in writings about political life: "The reason is that the way one ought to live is so far from how one does live, that anyone who leaves behind what one does for what one ought to do"—his wording is important here—"comes to understand his own 'ruin' rather than his 'preservation.'"[14] Short and lapidary—what he means by "ruin" (the Italian *ruina*) is the loss of power by the notional prince. And what he means by "preservation" (*preservazione*) is the prince's ability to keep his regime secure. Do not do what you "ought" to do. Do instead what "is done." "Because a man who wants in all things to make a show of being good will come to 'ruin' among so many who are not good."[15]

"Good," "bad." Again, Machiavelli brings things to their most elemental level. Later he will go into typologies of virtues and vices, but here, when he is making his point most effectively, he is outside of the university classroom, where countless thinkers before him offered extensive study of virtues and vices. Here, it is important that the main message come through: "it is necessary for a prince who wants to maintain himself to learn how not to be good and to use that ability or not according to what the situation requires."[16] This is the world as it is: seeming is more important than being, if one wants to maintain power.

Take the issue of keeping promises, the subject of chapter eighteen in *The Prince*. It might seem like a praiseworthy thing for a prince to keep his promises. "Still, in our day experience shows us that those princes who have accomplished great things have had few scruples about keeping promises."[17] There are two types of necessary political struggle: one involves laws, the other forces. Laws are particular to human beings, force is particular to animals, or "beasts," as Machiavelli puts it, and a prince needs to know how to use both natures. Machiavelli does not have a "philosophy of human nature." But in the world as it is, it is clear that people can be fooled: "men are so simple and they are so in thrall to what is most immediately important that anyone who wants to fool someone will always find someone willing to be fooled."[18]

A real life example for Machiavelli would be Pope Alexander VI, Cesare Borgia's father, who "did not think of anything else than how to fool people," or Ferdinand the Catholic (of

"Ferdinand and Isabella"), who "does nothing other than preach peace and the keeping of promises, even though he is most hostile to both—and had he observed both, there is more than one occasion on which he would have lost his state."[19] The truth is that a prince does need to seem—and it is good to be—"compassionate, trustworthy, humane, a person of integrity, and religious." But "your spirit has to be so inclined that, when the situation demands it, you can, and know how to, become the contrary. . . . Everyone sees what you seem to be. Few understand what you really are."[20] The world in reality is full of people going about their everyday lives who can see little else but what is right in front of them. A true leader must be able to do much more, to reach further, to outguess people's everyday expectations.

This brings us to the next of Machiavelli's characteristic concerns: the power of individuals. "No one should be surprised if, when I come to speak of princedoms that are entirely new and of princes and of states, I bring very great examples to bear."[21] What Machiavelli means here, at the beginning of his chapter six, is something he fleshes out later in chapter fourteen, when he discusses how a prince should behave with regard to military matters. He should read histories, and "he should consider in them the actions of outstanding men." Alexander the Great imitated the mythical Greek hero Achilles, Julius Caesar imitated Alexander, and the Roman general Scipio imitated the ancient Persian ruler Cyrus.[22] Machiavelli means, here and elsewhere, that to be effective leaders need to have before them examples they can cultivate, whether these examples are drawn from life experience or from the annals of history. We have lost this sense somewhat today, in our hyperindividualistic culture, where being "original" is so prized. But for Machiavelli, although history is permeated by instability, it is also marked by recognizable patterns. That notion, that there are patterns in history, combined with Machiavelli's belief that there are certain universal human traits and behaviors, leads him to surmise that imitating the strategies, habits, and actions of great men can and should inform leaders, even as a prospective prince should learn to avoid those characteristics that can lead him into ruin.

But it is not that individuals are cogs in the wheel of a perfectly predictable, lumbering machine. Nothing is completely foreordained. One of the book's most famous chapters, the twenty-fifth, is entitled "How much power fortune has in human affairs and how one is to respond to fortune." Machiavelli writes: "I am well aware that there are many who have been and who are of the opinion that worldly affairs are governed in some fashion by fortune and by God, and that men, even with their own prudence, cannot themselves govern, or even alter worldly affairs."[23] Some even go so far as to think that nothing can be done and that everything should be left to chance. "This opinion has gained more adherents in our own day, because of the momentous changes that have appeared and that appear every day, beyond any human imagining. At times, thinking about these matters, I myself have even inclined toward this opinion."[24] This is the world in which we find ourselves, Machiavelli suggests: a world of momentous changes, where political instability is the rule rather than the exception. In his own lifetime, he had seen French soldiers march through his city, had endured what was practically a religious dictatorship in the years of Savonarola, and then had been an active participant in the next government, that of Soderini, only to see it fall under pressure by powerful outside forces. And that is just Florence we are talking about. The rest of Italy was even worse.

How can one resist fortune? How can individuals have any real power to act, let alone to rule, that is not either preordained or subject to fortune's ever-spinning wheel? Before answering, it is worth opening a parenthesis on Machiavelli's views about God. First of all, he mentions God in the passage we have just seen. And God does appear, here and there, in Machiavelli's writing. But the real reason to think for a moment about Machiavelli and God is to foreground this fact: God is unimportant to Machiavelli. He is no atheist, needless to say, an identity that was foreign to his era. He simply brackets God and, to an extent, religion, whenever they come up, as he finds ways in his language to write God out of the picture. He might use the lightest of ironies to do this. In this chapter on fortune, for example, he wants to make the overall point that a ruler should worry about what he can control. He says that "in order that our free will not be extinguished, I judge that it may be true that fortune is the arbiter of half of our actions, but that it also lets us govern the other half, for the most part, ourselves."[25] Is he making a theological statement about free will? No. But in a chapter that began by invoking the belief of some people that God or fortune controls all our affairs, this is a reasonable way to make his main point: you should realize that instability and unpredictability exist in life, but you should not be paralyzed by those things and should instead act, in so far as you can, with expedition.

One might highlight chapter eleven, "On ecclesiastical princedoms," where again Machiavelli employs a mild variety of irony. He is dealing quite obviously with the papacy, but as he begins the chapter he makes it clear that he is talking about "ecclesiastical princedoms," plural. They are similar to others in that they are acquired by either fortune or virtue, but they are different, in that "they are maintained without either, since they are supported by the ancient orders of religion, which have been so powerful and are of such a sort that they hold their princes in power however they behave and live."[26] Popes are guaranteed to keep their jobs, Machiavelli is saying. They cannot be ousted. "Only these princes"—popes, in other words—"have states and do not defend them, have subjects and do not govern them," and yet despite this fact and unlike other princedoms, these are secure. "But since they are governed by higher causes at which the human mind cannot arrive, I will leave off speaking about them, because, since they are supported by God, discussing them would be the action of a presumptuous and rash man."[27]

But what is the first word of the next sentence? "Nevertheless." Nevertheless, Machiavelli says, he will at least discuss how the church became so prominent in temporal matters. And in doing so—in retailing the behavior of Alexander VI and then of Julius II as if he were discussing the cases of any other prince—Machiavelli communicates, not so indirectly, that much "disorder" has been caused in Italy by the presence of the papacy and—returning to God—that God can simply be left out of the discussion, even here, even when the discussion is revolving around the papacy. Special though it is, its political role can be discussed and understood in purely human terms.

Or take chapter six, which has to do with "new princedoms that are acquired with one's own arms" (by "arms" Machiavelli means one's own soldiers, in other words a military force under one's own power). Here Machiavelli focuses on "new" princedoms—by which he means those that are not hereditary—and how certain key individuals have fared. The leaders he discusses are ancient. Two are mythical, to an extent: Theseus, who fought with the Minotaur and founded Athens, and Romulus, who, abandoned as a child and suckled by a she-wolf along with his twin brother Remus, went on, after a fatal quarrel with Remus, to found the city of Rome. Then there was Cyrus, whose story Machiavelli knew from Herodotus, who relates that Cyrus, also abandoned as a child though of royal birth, went on to found the Persian Empire. But the most interesting figure Machiavelli discusses is Moses. "And even if one should not discuss Moses with human reason alone, since he was a mere executor of matters ordained by God, even still he should be admired, if only because he possessed the kind of grace that allowed him to talk with God."[28] Fair enough. Machiavelli brackets Moses, and he says enough to let readers know that he is aware that Moses is of a different order. Or does he? The immediately succeeding quotation offers a clue as to Machiavelli's intention: "If you consider Cyrus and the others who acquired or founded kingdoms, you will find them all to be sources of wonder."[29] Having differentiated Moses from the other examples, Machiavelli here brings him closer. And then Machiavelli goes on to say that, if one considers their actions and the way these leaders carried out and regulated their state-building enterprises, those things "will not seem all that different from those of Moses, who"—and here is the key—"had such a great teacher."[30]

With God or without God, great men will perform great actions, but only on one condition: that they have the right "chance."[31] The word Machiavelli uses for "chance" is the Italian *occasione*, which is itself drawn directly from the Latin, *occasio*, a word that has a parallel in the ancient Greek, *kairos*. It means, really, not just a chance, but the right chance, a moment imbued with potential if only the person facing that moment seizes it boldly. Moses found the Israelites enslaved and oppressed by the Egyptians. Cyrus found the Persians discontented under the rule of the Medes and found the Medes soft and weak owing to long peace. And so on. To close the parenthesis, then: each great leader has a chance, but he must recognize that chance and pursue it. It is ultimately his choice whether and how to pursue these opportunities. It is not up to God.

Returning to fortune and individual action, it is clear that Machiavelli does believe that "fortune" exists, otherwise how to explain all the instability with which his city, not to mention the rest of Italy, has been surrounded? It is easier for him to say what fortune is "like," rather than saying what it is. "It is like one of those rough rivers that, when it overflows, floods the plains, ruins trees and buildings," and so on.[32] Powerful as these rivers may be, people can do things in times of tranquil weather: they can build stronger embankments and shelters that can withstand rough rivers. "Fortune intervenes in just this fashion, exercising its powers where there is not adequate strength to resist it." This is Italy's problem, by the way: "If you look at Italy, which has been the seat of all of these changes recently, you will see that it is a countryside without embankments and shelter." If only Italy had been like "Germany" (Machiavelli means more or less the Swiss), Spain, and France, "then this flood would not have caused such momentous changes as it has done, or might not even have occurred."[33]

As to individuals and their actions, they need first of all to learn to adapt. That prince remains *felice*—happy, fortunate, remaining in power in other words—who finds his conduct in conformity with the times. Still, the same conduct does not always produce the same results. This is why you sometimes see two people, "proceeding in different fashions, producing the same effect, and two people proceeding in the same fashion, and one reaches his goal and the other does not."[34] No one can be so prudent as to foresee everything, people do have different natures, and they tend to do what their nature inclines them to do. "The cautious man, when it is time for him to be impetuous, does not know how to do it and is thus ruined."[35] The reverse can also be true. Fortune and its relation to individual action remain a textured mystery, a fabric whose skeins Machiavelli continues to unravel.

As always, he has examples to relate. The most prominent of these is Pope Julius II, who occupied the chair of St. Peter from 1503 to 1513. Today he is perhaps best known for his stormy association with Michelangelo, as he had commissioned the great Florentine artist to decorate the ceiling of the Sistine Chapel and occasionally clashed with him about the calendar for its completion. Julius was also a notable patron of the artist Raphael. But Machiavelli is not interested in art. Instead, he highlights Julius's impetuousness and the way in which he threw himself into political and military affairs: "Pope Julius II acted impetuously in every one of his actions, and he found both the times and affairs of his day so well matched to his way of proceeding that he always happened upon a good outcome."[36] In the complex maneuvers that different powers were then undertaking—as the Bolognese, the Venetians, the king of

Spain and the king of France were all vying for an advantage—Julius himself entered into the field of battle, accompanied by his own troops. This was so surprising that it stopped the Venetians and the Spanish from moving forward and convinced the French to ally with Julius. And so, "with his impetuous move, Julius achieved what no other pope, with all possible human prudence, would have done. The reason is that, had he waited to leave Rome until all agreements had been concluded and everything well-ordered, as any other pope would have done, he never would have succeeded, since the French king would have had a thousand excuses and the others would have put forward a thousand fears."[37] Machiavelli simultaneously describes Julius's bold actions as commendable in this instance and implicitly criticizes other popes as too indecisive. But he is careful to conclude his discussion of Julius by stressing that in this case Julius's natural, bold temperament happened to match the times. "Had there emerged times that required him to proceed with caution, his ruin would have followed, since he would never have changed the way he proceeded from the way nature inclined him to do."[38]

Machiavelli's repetitiveness here—the way he continues to remind his reader that things work out for the best only if a prince's natural habits align well with the times he faces—seems to discomfit even him for a bit. So he ends this famous chapter on fortune with one of the most famous—and to modern ears most disturbing—images in *The Prince*, making a recommendation that, even though uncertainty will always exist, in general, "it is better to be impetuous rather than cautious, since fortune is a woman, and it is necessary, if you want to have her, to strike her and force her to your will. One sees that fortune lets herself be conquered more by those who are impetuous than by those who proceed coolly and that, like a woman, she is a friend to young men, since they are less cautious, fiercer, and they control her more boldly."[39] Machiavelli's point here is to reiterate, at the end of his chapter, something he comments on elsewhere and that indeed was proverbial even in antiquity: "fortune favors the bold." There will come a time to comment on the fact that Machiavelli can be, in the context of his own time, quite tactless, addressing rulers and notable people with more frankness than appropriate. This is not one of those times, and it reminds us that, for all the ways we can see "modern" habits of thought in Machiavelli, he lived, in a western context, in a premodern world, one of frequent gender separation, where the concept of human rights did not exist. No one among his contemporary readers would have batted an eye that his choice of metaphor involved an analogy to rape.

This would be a good time to move to Machiavelli's thoughts about how a prince should wield power, since here too we are operating in a world where brute force took pride of place. "Arms"—*le arme* in Italian—appear again and again in Machiavelli's work, *The Prince* very much included. For Machiavelli, this term comprises mainly the military forces a prince, in this instance, has at his command. But he also means by it "military affairs" in general, and there lies behind his focus on "arms" a fundamental Machiavellian rule about political power: having military power is most important. Having gone through his typology of different princedoms, he suggests that a prince needs most of all to have good "foundations." Good foundations consist principally in good laws and good "arms." "And since there cannot be good laws where there are not good arms, and where there are good arms it makes sense to have good laws, I will leave behind discussion about laws and talk about arms."[40] This sentiment is important in understanding where Machiavelli is coming from. During his own career, Machiavelli helped make laws and statutes in the different offices he held at different times. But the paramount importance of military power is what guides his writing. Machiavelli does not assume, in other words, that a certain form of government will of necessity lead to a more flourishing society. Instead any form of government, to be stable (the mirror image of what Machiavelli saw all around him, in other words), needs a strong military foundation.

As many had done before him, Machiavelli deplores the use of mercenaries, soldiers under the command of an independent military captain working for pay, rather than for love of country. They fight for nothing other than *un poco di stipendio*—"a little bit of money," which—Machiavelli goes on—"is not enough to make them want to die for you."[41] The military captains, or *condottieri*, always and without exception represent danger: if they are unskilled, they are obviously useless, whereas if they are talented, "you cannot trust them, since they will always seek to aggrandize themselves, either by subjugating you or by subjugating others outside of your intentions."[42] Mercenaries are motivated by nothing other than money.

"Auxiliaries" are just as bad. By this term Machiavelli means that state of affairs in which a prince from one state allies with another for the express purpose of having the partner's military prowess. The emperor of Constantinople did this when he invited ten thousand Turks into Greece. "But once the war was over, they did not want to leave, which was the beginning of Greece's servitude to the infidels."[43] Machiavelli is referring to a mid-fourteenth century episode, when the Byzantine Emperor John IV Kantakouzenos was engaged in a war against his rival John V Palaiologos. Kantakouzenos requested and received aid from the Turkish emir, Orhan, who sent a substantial force captained by his son, who thereafter occupied Gallipoli on the European side of the Dardanelles, marking the first Turkish, and Muslim, possession near Greece. This incursion was thus a predecessor to the Fall of Constantinople in 1453 and, for Machiavelli (in his currently politically incorrect version), the beginning of Greece's "servitude to the infidel." But the devil is not in the details here. The main point regarding auxiliaries is simply this: "whoever does not want to win, choose these arms, since they are much more dangerous than mercenaries."[44] With them the foundation of conspiracy is already laid: you have thousands of troops on your own territory whose basic loyalty is to someone else. If you lose with their aid, you have suffered your loss anyway. If you win with their aid, you remain under the sway of the ruler who furnished them.

Overall, "in mercenaries it is their lack of will that is the most dangerous, in auxiliaries, it is their virtue."[45] Machiavelli winds up his discussion this way: "I therefore conclude that, without having its own arms, no princedom is safe, indeed it is instead totally tied to fortune, having no virtue that during times of adversity can defend it with trustworthiness; and it has always been the opinion and sentiment of wise men"—and here Machiavelli breaks into Latin, paraphrasing a respected ancient author, Tacitus—*quod nihil sit tam infirmum aut instabile quam fama potentiae non sua vi nixa*—"that there is nothing so weak and unstable as a reputation for power that is not founded on

its own force."[46] This sentiment and others like it are repeated
so often in Machiavelli's work that it is practically de rigueur
for him to mention it. Here as elsewhere, one sees a critique of
everything by which he sees himself surrounded and, retrospectively, a justification of his own work on the Florentine military and the reconquest of Pisa, his greatest success as a public
servant and the proudest moment of his career. But Machiavelli was tilting at windmills, at least in a practical sense. He
lived in a country that was not yet a country, a state with no
real constitution, and an environment in which regional and
personal loyalties mattered far more than the notionally "national" spirit toward which he was pointing, if ever so incho-
ately. Other countries and other leaders would learn more, and
sooner, from Machiavelli's advice about citizen and subject
armies than would his fellow Italians.[47]

But let us say a prince did follow Machiavelli's advice regarding having his own "arms." What then should this prince's
attitude be toward military affairs? Here again, Machiavelli
launches implicit critiques, the likes of which come up again
in his other work. First, one should never postpone a war, if it
will at some point become necessary anyway. The ancient Romans were wise, "because they knew that wars are not avoided,
they are only put off, to the advantage of others . . . one must
never allow disorder to occur only to flee a war."[48] Machiavelli
believed this tendency to delay inevitable conflict could be fatal
to a state, and he was convinced that his fellow Florentines had
succumbed to this temptation far too often.

A prince's one primary responsibility, that to which he should
dedicate all his efforts, all the time, is to prepare for war: "The
prince must have no other object, no other thought, and take

nothing else as his own art outside the art of war, both its rules and in training for it."[49] Only the art of war can maintain a prince in power who was born to his princedom, and the art of war has the power to raise someone up from status as a private citizen to that of a prince. "And on the other hand, one sees that those princes who have thought more about living a life of luxury than about arms have lost their state."[50] Machiavelli goes on immediately thereafter to enunciate precisely why it is important for a prince to be "armed," in one of the most striking passages in the entire book: "Among other reasons that can cause you harm, being unarmed makes you despised, which is one of those indignities that a prince must studiously avoid . . . because between an armed and an unarmed man there is no comparison, and it does not stand to reason that someone who is armed will willingly obey someone unarmed or that someone unarmed will be safe among those who serve him who are armed."[51] The category "those who serve him" also includes military captains, for Machiavelli, who is saying here, again, that no prince can consider himself safe who is relying on paid outsiders for military support. But it is also worth noting that the link between arms and power is remarkably durable. Most U.S. presidents have served in the military, and for those who have not, lack of service often proves a liability in the quest to become commander in chief.

So we know enough to realize that Machiavelli thinks military affairs are important. But he has further, concrete pieces of advice for a prince. The first is that he should spend a great deal of time hunting. Doing so, he will learn about the lie not only of his own lands but also analogous ones, since hills, valleys, plains, rivers, and so on bear similarities from province to province. The prince should also study history and the actions of great men. As always Machiavelli has an example at the ready, this time of Philopomen (general of the Achaean league in the late third and early second centuries BC, about whom Machiavelli read in his favorite historian, Livy), who would go on scouting expeditions with his men and ask them things like "if the enemy were on that hill and we were here with our army, who would have the advantage over us? How could we go to encounter them while still preserving battle formation?"—and so on.[52] In general, a wise prince should "never be at leisure during times of peace, but rather profit from that time to be able to be strong during adversity. This way when fortune changes direction, you will find him prepared to resist it."[53] As always, we feel the energy of Machiavelli's agile mind, as he chews questions over, switching from second person to third person, repeating his sentiments in different ways and with varied examples, and ultimately putting the most emphasis where he thinks it belongs: on the prince's need to care first and foremost about his relation to "arms."

It is worth noting that much of *The Prince* concerns descriptions of qualities a prince should possess, rather than strategies. These descriptions also include qualities to avoid, and the worst of these are being "despised"—*contennendo* in Italian—and being *odioso*—"hated." Having the right sorts of qualities represents another way to wield power and command assent. All of his recommendations, again, have to do with the world as it is, rather than as it could be. Though being miserly is a negative quality, the truth is that having a mild reputation for miserliness is better than being overly generous—generosity takes money, and gaining money means taxing your subjects, and taxing your subjects can make you hated. And being too generous also means you run the risk of running out of money, a condition that can lead to your being despised. Being deemed miserly, on the other hand, means that every act of generosity that you do perform will seem even more generous, because exceptional.[54] So guard your resources well, and do not make big displays of wealth.

Then there is the classic question related to power—is it better to be loved or feared?—a question bound up with the qualities of "cruelty" and "mercy."[55] On the one hand, Cesare Borgia had a reputation for great cruelty. On the other, look how successful he was. A prince should not fear a reputation for cruelty, since with a few well chosen cruel acts, he can avoid "disorders" from which violent deaths inevitably ensue. These deaths in a sense manifest "cruelty" to a whole set of people, rather than to only one individual. An earlier chapter related how Borgia, in trying to control the Romagna region, put a man named Remirro d'Orca—"a man cruel and quick"—in charge of the town of Cesena, who by acts of brutality reduced a disordered place to order. But then Borgia came to believe that such excessive authority was not useful anymore, fearing it might cause him to be hated. Borgia wanted the people, who were becoming restive, to believe that, if any excessive acts of cruelty had occurred, these were due to Remirro's violent nature, rather than to Borgia. "So . . . one morning Borgia had him divided into two pieces right in the piazza, with a piece of wood and a bloody knife next to him. The brutality of that spectacle both satisfied and stunned the people."[56]

The truth is that you can perform cruel acts "well" or "poorly," something that more than once leads Machiavelli into sustained reflection. In the eighth chapter (when he is still in the midst of his typology of princedoms), Machiavelli discusses those who came to power through "evil acts," using some choice ancient and modern examples. There is Agathocles the Sicilian, who ruled Syracuse from 316 to 289 BC and who, though low born, rose to great power by engaging in vicious and cruel acts, none more so than when he summoned the Senate and people of Syracuse, ostensibly for a political discussion. No sooner had the party arrived than he had his soldiers murder all the senators and the richest and most prominent citizens (Machiavelli's main source for this story is the enigmatic ancient historian Justin, writing during the Roman imperial period, who preserved excerpts from a much broader history written earlier by Pompeius Trogus). Now it is true, Machiavelli suggests, that "one cannot call it 'virtue' to murder one's own citizens, betray friends, be faithless, merciless, and without religious scruples" and that Agathocles should not be celebrated among the "most outstanding men" worthy of imitation.[57] But Machiavelli is nonetheless fascinated by Agathocles' personal will, referring to his *virtù di animo e di corpo*—his "strength of spirit and body"—and to the *grandezza dello animo suo*—"his greatness of spirit."[58] Again we are reminded how important personal characteristics and individual will are to Machiavelli.

So if one returns to the question whether it is better to be loved or feared and how this problem relates to the symbolic implementation of power, these considerations should always be in the background. Put simply, Machiavelli will give rules and strategies, but they are always to be matched to an individual's nature. The first thing we learn is that "it is much safer to be feared than loved."[59] The reason? "Because, of men one can say this, generally speaking: that they are ungrateful, fickle, fakers and liars, inclined to flee danger, desirous of financial gain." When things are going well, they "are all yours, and offer you their blood, property, life, and their children," but when things are going poorly and the need for their help is upon you, they are nowhere to be found.[60] Does Machiavelli here evince a negative view of "human nature"? Not necessarily. After all, he is talking about politics and is drawing on long observation, as well as his own, not so felicitous, life experience. Perhaps we can say that, in his view, a prince needs to assume these things about people—their fickleness and so on—since a prince who wants to gain and maintain power needs to focus on what he can control. Military matters come first, above all, and always. But when it comes to being loved or feared, one can much more easily control being feared: "men are less cautious about going against someone who tries to make himself loved than against someone who makes himself feared."[61]

The important thing is to be feared, but not in such a way that you are hated. This is easy enough to do, and Machiavelli tells you how. "This will always occur, provided one stays away from the property of one's citizens and subjects as well as their women. And if it becomes necessary to inflict physical violence on someone, one must do it only when there is a reasonable justification and a clear cause."[62] This matter of property is so important to Machiavelli that he goes into the issue at even greater length: "But most of all it is necessary to stay away from the property of others, because men will sooner forget the death of their father than the loss of their patrimony; moreover, there will always be reasons to take away property, and it always happens that whoever begins to make a living by theft, always finds a reason to take other people's things away."[63] These passages are worth extended reflection.

First, as to the women: this commonplace notion has a long history, reaching back to Aristotle (whom Machiavelli cites for this view in another work).[64] Much of this is about honor and masculine virtue and the sense that if a man cannot protect his women he is less of a man, and so on. More interesting, however, is the notion of property, as Machiavelli twice says that you must "stay away from the property of others." The word Machiavelli uses in Italian, translated here (and traditionally) as "property," is *roba*, which in its most literal sense means something like "stuff" or "things." It is important to highlight this fact, because again we encounter Machiavelli in his own, premodern time, and we do so by listening carefully to what he says. He is not setting forth a "theory of private property." Rather, he is simply observing that, in general, rulers fare poorly when they take other people's things. People are aware, he suggests elsewhere, that when someone dies, even a family member, one cannot bring that person back to life. But property, a farm, say, can always be imagined as being regained: "everyone knows that, with a change of state"—Machiavelli means here a change in government and therefore a change in ruler—"one cannot bring a brother back to life, but one can very well have his farm back."[65]

So cruel acts have their place, but like every other princely action, they must be calibrated against what the times require and what people habitually tolerate. The only exception to this relatively moderate outlook occurs when Machiavelli considers a prince who is in the field with his army. In that case, without a reputation for cruelty among his soldiers he will "never hold the army united or inclined toward a military operation."[66] In the final analysis, "since being loved depends on the people and being feared depends on the prince, a wise prince must found his actions on what is his, rather than on what belongs to others."[67]

This notion that you must behave according to what you can control is particularly apt when considering another factor that runs through all of Machiavelli's work: a profound consciousness of instability. This consciousness is everywhere, in the obsessive highlighting in *The Prince* of the differences between the ideal and the real, in his fascination with history, in his deliberations on fortune and on what individuals can and cannot control, and most of all in the world in which Machiavelli found himself. For all the uncertainties, potential conspiracies, and battles experienced in the late fifteenth century, the truth was that Florence had not seen anything like the period after 1494, when the French king Charles VIII marched through the city and Savonarola's tumultuous political career was born, dying dramatically along with him in a public execution. And then, finally, despite Machiavelli and his cohort's best-laid plans, the city found itself once more in the hands of the Medici, this time supported by outside powers. This, anyway, is what Machiavelli saw, and as he was composing *The Prince*, confined in his country home outside of Florence, instability was what he pondered, what he had experienced most profoundly in his own life.

In *The Prince*, this consciousness of instability most clearly stands out in a peculiar and fascinating chapter, the twentieth, which concerns "whether fortresses and other things that princes do are useful or not useful." Princes have done many things to hold on to power. Some have disarmed their subjects, thinking this would guarantee civic peace, whereas others have encouraged factions in their subject territories, believing in a sort of divide and conquer strategy. Some have nourished enmities against themselves, thinking that having an enemy to conquer offered a mission and a goal to themselves and their allies, whereas others have tried to win over those who had, at the outset of their princedom, seemed to be enemies. Still others have built fortresses, whereas others destroyed them.

This chapter, like many in *The Prince*, is chock full of historical and contemporary examples. But what is most striking about it is the delicate play between instability and the attempts to tame it (since it cannot be defeated) through observation. It is as if, somehow, the use and charting of different examples could at least serve as a buttress against history and its inevitable uncertainties: "even though it is impossible to offer a complete account of all these things"—taking away subjects' arms, fortresses, and so on—"without entering into the particular circumstances of those states where you would need to make a decision, nevertheless"—here is that "nevertheless" again—"I will speak in a manner as broad as the matter admits."[68]

When Machiavelli comes to the issue of fortresses, ambivalence emerges: "It has been the custom of princes, in order to hold their states more securely, to build fortresses, like a bridle and a bit against those who might move against them, and also to have secure refuge from a sudden attack. I approve of this way of doing things since it has been used since antiquity."[69] Nevertheless, in modern times, there are a number of successful princes who have taken pains to destroy fortresses on their territories. Therefore, "fortresses are useful, or not, according to the times. If they help you on one hand, they harm you on the other."[70] The real guideline is this: "a prince who is more afraid of the people than of foreigners should build fortresses, but he who has more fear of foreigners should leave them behind."[71] The key, as ever, is to endeavor not to be hated by the people. Machiavelli concludes the chapter as follows: "All things considered, I will praise someone who builds fortresses as well as someone who does not, and I will blame whoever trusts in fortresses but thinks that being hated by the people is of little importance."[72]

The rest of *The Prince* details other ways in which a prince can secure his position. Should a citizen do something extraordinary, whether positive or negative, the prince should recognize it, by rewarding or punishing the citizen in a way "that people will talk about a lot."[73] A prince is also well esteemed when "he is a true friend and a true enemy."[74] In other words, do not stay neutral if your neighbors are in conflict with one another. Pick a side. If you do not, neither will trust you, and when the fighting is over, you will have to fear the winner, and the loser will feel no affection for you. But if you pick a side, and if your side has won, you will have a strong ally. If your side has lost, you will at least have the trust and esteem of the loser, and you can rise again together. Decisiveness is important. Florence was hurt, Machiavelli suggests, by not participating in Julius II's Holy League, which united papal and other Italian forces with Spain against the French, and by not being anything more than a lukewarm ally of France.

The prince can also win esteem and avoid being hated by the people by recognizing even the humblest orders of citizens and by putting on festivals and spectacles and therein offering examples of his humanity and munificence (provided he maintains his dignity). A prince should have good advisors, who respect him and think of his welfare first but whom he can trust enough to allow them to speak their minds freely.[75] And he should avoid flatterers, who are found everywhere in courts.[76]

Surrounded by instability as he was, Machiavelli, in *The Prince*—a treatise that in addition to being a kind of job application to the newly installed Medici was also an exhortation—had to present strategies that he thought would work. So as the work winds towards its end, Machiavelli seems decisive, more so than he probably was in his heart of hearts. The princes of Italy have lost their states because (he suggests in chapter twenty-four) when times were good, they never anticipated that things might change.[77] And most shameful of all, when bad times came, many of them simply fled, believing that the people in their respective cities would be so angered by the arrogance of the conqueror that they would call the exiled princes back. But again, Italian princes trusted too much in matters they could not control.

The final chapter, twenty-six, is *The Prince's* most hortatory, tellingly titled "An exhortation to take Italy in hand and to win back her liberty from the barbarians." To understand this chapter—its guiding spirit, Machiavelli's goals, his hopes and dreams as manifested therein—it is enough to quote its final lines, which themselves represent a quotation:

> *Virtù contro a furore*
> *prenderà l'armi, e fia el combatter corto,*
> *che l'antico valore*
> *nelli italici cor non è ancor morto.*

[Virtue will take up arms
against fury, and may the fighting be short,
since the ancient strength
in Italian hearts is not yet dead.]

The quotation Machiavelli chooses to end *The Prince* comes from another notable Florentine, Francesco Petrarca, Petrarch, who before his death in 1374 became one of the Renaissance's key revivers of ancient Latin style and, along the way, one of its best known vernacular poets. The poem from which Machiavelli cites is *Italia mia*—"My Italy."[78] It reflects, as do other works of Petrarch, a longing, infused by rose-hued memories of ancient glory and power, to see a united Italy, powerful once again, from which "foreigners" would be expelled.

Machiavelli's final chapter breathes that same rarified air, that hope, long gone, that somehow, some way, Italy's vastly diverse, culturally self-conscious city-states could come together under a unified purpose. That purpose, for Machiavelli, would be shaped by a new prince, who could profit from the widespread disgust Machiavelli believes that all Italians feel for the outsized foreign presence on Italian soil.[79] "What people would deny their obedience? . . . What Italian would deny him their compliance? To everyone, this barbarous dominion stinks," Machiavelli says, in his salty, premodern way.[80]

Unifying Italy. In 1513. When Italy has repeatedly been overrun by foreign armies, and Italy's city-states are being used as pawns in the political chess games of the powerful. Is Machiavelli a dreamer, a utopian? Is it a coincidence that, at almost the exact same time Machiavelli was working on *The Prince*, Thomas More wrote his *Utopia*, a work that saw the light in

1516—well before More was executed for his beliefs in 1535—
and became a best-selling description of a perfectly functioning,
imagined, small state, where the right organization provided
for its inhabitants a life of ease, reflection, and what we would
today call "wellness"? Needless to say, as Renaissance thinkers
recovered ancient texts (Plato's *Republic* among them), there was
a temptation to try to sketch out models of ideal states. More's
title, *Utopia*, is a combination of two Greek words: *ou*, a prefix
that means "no," and *topos*, which means "place." More's *Utopia*
is "no place," something that its author cleverly titled as such,
as a model that he knew could never be achieved. Hindsight
permits us to recognize that Machiavelli's dream—or, as we
might rather call it, trial balloon—that Italy could be unified
under a strong prince was destined not to succeed in his day.
Still, we should give the secretary a break: he was writing what
amounted to a job application after having been arrested and
tortured. He wanted, as ever, to find some way to get back into
government and be useful to his city.

But there is one more reason why we should excuse Machiavelli his effervescent bout of dreaming, and this has, once again,
to do with instability. The message of *The Prince* is that no one
can prescribe exact political techniques that will work at all
times. One can instead use examples drawn from history and
personal observation, prepare for war in times of peace, and
finally—when it comes to instability—realize that there will
always be conflict. This latter point, stressing the unavoidable
reality of conflict, is worth highlighting. Machiavelli is not only
saying that wars will always be with us, with all their prospective instability, and that the possibility for external conflict is
ever present. Machiavelli is also saying that internal conflict,

within a state, will always be there, as different segments of society vie for power, recognition, and protection of their interests.

Take what he says about how and when a "private citizen," which is to say someone who was not hitherto involved in government, becomes prince of his homeland with the favor of his fellow citizens.[81] This transition occurs "either with the favor of the people or with the favor of the great," meaning that this citizen is raised up either because his elevation is desired and supported by the "people"—Machiavelli means here something like middle-class merchants—or by the "great," the *grandi*—by which Machiavelli means, essentially, aristocrats (whether titled or not depends on the local traditions of the city). The reason it happens this way is that in general you will find two "humors"—*umori* (here and elsewhere Machiavelli uses medical language familiar to his Renaissance readers, a usage that should not be taken too seriously, being rather in the nature of metaphor than science): "the people desire not to be subject and oppressed by the great, and the great desire to subject and to oppress the people."[82] The man raised up in either of these two ways—with the favor of the people or with that of the aristocrats—will have his own problems. If he was elevated by the aristocrats, he will have difficulties because they see everyone as their equals, and if by the people, he will find himself alone and always needing to maintain their favor. Typical Machiavelli—difficulties all around.

But what is important here is not the specific situation at hand but rather the notion that there is built-in conflict in every state. Nowhere is this truer than in republics, which have more constituencies to satisfy, more potentially powerful factions, and more voices demanding to be heard.

Was Machiavelli more predisposed to favor one-man rule (as *The Prince* might lead us to believe), or was he more in favor of "republics" as a means of organizing society? His *Discourses on Livy* can help us piece together an answer to this question. As always with Machiavelli, the answer turns out to be surprising.

5

Conversing with the Ancients

In republics there is more life, more hatred, more desire for revenge.
—MACHIAVELLI, *The Prince*, chapter five

✦　✦　✦

Republics serve as the center of Machiavelli's reflection in his *Discourses on Livy*, the other great work, alongside *The Prince*, on which he was engaged during his time on the farm but which he brought to fruition only later. Each work has cross-references to the other, so we know Machiavelli was working on them, at least in part, at more or less the same time, inevitably concentrating more energies for a time on *The Prince*, since he so hoped to find a way back into government and since the Medici had just come back into power.

The full title of the *Discourses* is *Discourses on the First Decade of Livy*, a title whose terms deserve some explanation. The first of these is "Livy." Though he is ancient Rome's most famous historian, we know so little about Livy that we lack even a *cognomen* for him. This Latin word signifies, effectively, a last name—Cicero's full Latin name was Marcus Tullius Cicero, Julius Caesar's was Gaius Julius Caesar, and so on. All we know of Livy's Latin name is "Titus Livius." And we know from other evidence that he came from Padua, near Venice, and from still other evidence that he was born most likely in 59 BC and died in 17 AD. Livy was in Rome during its most dramatic moments, having become acquainted with Octavian, the eventual winner in the struggles that featured players like Mark Antony and Cleopatra. Octavian, Livy's patron, would become Rome's first emperor and take the name Augustus. But we know the most about Livy from his monumental, instantly famous work of history, called simply *Ab urbe condita*—"From the Founding of the City"—"the City" meaning Rome. It was a gigantic work, comprising originally 142 "books," which were each much lengthier than chapters. Think of them as "novella"-sized, amounting to about 70–80 pages each. The work garnered great fame when it was released, with one contemporary said to have traveled all the way from Cadiz, in southwest Spain, just to meet its author.[1]

If its fame in Livy's own day and in the immediate centuries thereafter was great, Livy's *History*—like so much else in the manuscript era, when all books were hand-copied—fell victim to fortune's wheel. The *History* was transmitted in "decades," sets of ten books, and sometimes "pentads," or sets of five, according to Livy's own organization of the work. What this meant was that as scribes copied Livy's *History* using these guidelines, these sets would then circulate as separate collections. As readers in different eras and places understandably had different interests, some of Livy's *History* was preserved and some was not. Today, of the original 142 books, we possess only thirty-five (with an additional fragment of a thirty-sixth). And the reason we possess even as much was we do has to do in large part with Machiavelli's Renaissance predecessors, and most especially with Petrarch, who did admirable work reconstructing as much of the ancient text as he could find, scouring medieval libraries for different manuscript copies, comparing them to each other, and filling in missing sections in the text when he found them in different copies.[2]

A poignant episode from Machiavelli's youth: we learn from the diary of his father, the lawyer Bernardo Machiavelli, that Bernardo agreed in 1476 to prepare an index of place names to Livy, in return for which he would receive the printer's copy on which he worked. Ten years later we hear that Bernardo sent an unbound printed copy of Livy (perhaps the very same one) to a bookbinder (printers then set and printed the text, often delivered in unbound quires to the recipient, who would then send the book to a binder to be bound according to the desired specifications—lavishly, if one were rich, less so if one were not). "My young son Nicolò" was sent ten days later to pay the binder with a barrel of wine.[3] We see that Machiavelli, even when young, was exposed to Livy and that Livy's *History* had been so important in his family that his father saw fit to enter notes about it in his diary. So we can infer that Livy was a presence in Machiavelli's mind from a young age.

It is easy to see why Livy was appealing to Machiavelli, as he has been for so many other readers curious about ancient Rome. Livy wrote about exemplary people, about politics, and about war. Most importantly he wrote in the premodern world. Though there were countless differences and many centuries between their two worlds, there were enough basic, bedrock similarities for Livy's history to have a more immediate appeal for Machiavelli than it might have for us today. To understand these similarities, spending some time in Livy's delightful company is necessary.

The first of these similarities was in the conception of history: its possibilities, its principal techniques, and its utility. In his preface, Livy outlined his task, which was, simply, to cover everything, in a chronological sense, in the history of Rome. Doing so meant going back to the very beginning, to a time before history and infused with myth, when we hear of "charming things handed down in poetic tales rather than with solid proof."[4] Livy will relate these tales, for "antiquity can be pardoned if by mingling matters human and divine it makes the past seem more dignified, and if any people ought to be allowed to add sanctity to their origins, because of the glory of war, that privilege belongs to the Romans."[5] When it is possible to supply substantiated stories, Livy will do so. When not, he will still press on.

Livy continues: "More to the point, I urge the reader to consider the private lives and public morals of our ancestors, as well as how in politics and war they both acquired and grew Rome's power."[6] The main technique is episodic and takes for granted that individuals—their actions and character—represent history's primary focus. What else should Livy's ideal reader do? "I would then have him observe, as their principles weakened, which is to say as their morality evanesced, how they decayed ever more until the whole edifice collapsed and then finally how one has arrived to the point we are at now, when we can bear neither our vices nor the remedies that might cure them."[7] These are strong words, especially coming from a man writing during the time of Augustus, Rome's first emperor. But they also offer a template, a shape, and coherence to the story: in the distant past our ancestors were virtuous, simpler, contented with less. Of late, "wealth has brought greed, and too much sensual pleasure has brought a desire for luxury and, as it were, a lust for destruction, for losing all."[8] In the old days, in other words, moderation and virtue prevailed. Now, an excessive love of leisure, lives lived in the lap of luxury, and a weakening of the moral fiber have put both individuals and our nation at risk.

How many times have we heard this before? How many times do we hear it even now? Is it any surprise that the basic framework of virtuous beginnings, smart strategic expansion, and then decadence will also be Machiavelli's own basic framework when he looks at the history of Florence, whether in the *Discourses* or, years later, in his own *Florentine Histories?* As to Livy, a final sentiment, one that is often quoted, is worth repeating here. "It is this especially in the study of history that is healthy and profitable: you observe instances of every kind of conduct, a record clearly displayed from which you may select for yourself and your country what to imitate and from which you may avoid that which is shameful through and through."[9] History's primary purpose, for Livy, was to offer examples from the past of personal conduct and of policies that leaders of the present could follow or avoid. The basic assumptions—so basic that they did not need to be articulated—were these: few people will have the ability to comprehend historical argumentation. Those that do belong to the classes of people that we might term the elite—those who had the means and traditions needed to appreciate history and those who could read or follow something being read to them. Finally, these are the people called upon to rule, in normal circumstances. Again, as in the case of Machiavelli's own basic outline (virtuous origins, expansion, decadence), these assumptions about who his readers were likely to be were in force for Machiavelli as well.

And the first ten books of Livy's *History* were replete with memorable characters and episodes from Rome's beginnings to its emergence as a great power. Livy gave an account at the outset, in book 1, as he must, of Rome's semimythical founding, where he reconciled two traditions: first there was the originally Greek tale of Aeneas, the refugee from fallen Troy, who landed in Italy after many adventures and, because of his virtues both personal and martial, established himself in Italy, with his son Iulus going on to provide early rule. Then, there was the traditional Italian origin tale of the twin brothers, Romulus and Remus, abandoned at birth like many other legendary figures (Moses among them), raised early on by a humble farmer, and finally able to establish their originally royal birth. They came into conflict with one another, and then Romulus, having killed his brother, went on to be Rome's first King. Six others followed him, the last of whom, Tarquin the Proud, made himself so despised that the institution of kingship itself was abolished, and the Roman Republic was born. Rome's early history, including the period of the kings, takes up the lion's share of Livy's book 1.

Thereafter Livy details what seems almost constant war, as expansionist Rome comes into conflict with neighboring cities inhabited by people with their own languages and traditions. Along the way, there are the creations of signal institutions. After the kings, for instance, the Roman senate grew in power, two "consuls" were elected yearly, and, in order to give a voice to the "plebeians," who often came into conflict with the highest echelons of Rome's society, the office of "tribune of the people" was created. ("Plebeian" meant something different for Livy from what the word connotes in English today and is analogous to what Machiavelli meant when he used the word *popolo*, or "the people." Livy's plebeians, landholders but not aristocrats, form a lower order of society, understood implicitly as such, but they were still high enough on the social ladder to expect and be granted representation: think of shopkeepers, merchants, small landholders, and so on.) In addition to Rome's ever-present conflict with its neighbors, Livy also tells of conflict within the city: the biggest bone of contention was the distribution of land, since plebeians, especially those who had served in Rome's military (as most did), believed they were entitled to land. By the end of the first ten books (Machiavelli's special interest), Rome had conquered a number of surrounding peoples, consolidated its territories, and become a major regional power, with Livy taking his readers through the year 293 BC, as we would today reckon the date.

All of this sounds very reasonable: facts about Rome, portraits of leaders, heroes, and villains, notable legal developments in Rome's history, and so on. But reading closely, one cannot help but notice, as often occurs, what a different world we live in from that of Livy—and of Machiavelli. Take the story of the *Decemviri*, which occurs in book 3. Both the story itself and Machiavelli's reaction to it command sustained attention. This episode is enfolded in a larger narrative detailing the constantly evolving political struggles inside Rome, and takes place right around 450 BC. By this time, there were normally two consuls chosen yearly from among the patricians, which is to say the senatorial class and, effectively, the party of the elites. Since 494 BC the plebeians had gained the right to elect representatives whom they called *tribuni plebis*, "tribunes of the people." That year had seen the plebeians mount a strike, refusing to report for military service until this right of representation was granted. This labor action revealed the power of the plebeians, but it did not settle the conflict that continued to occur between these two orders.

After two leading Roman citizens were sent to Athens to study their laws, it was decided in 452 BC to appoint a commission of ten men, the *Decemviri*, who were charged with writing up laws for Rome that, it was hoped, would help give firmer foundations to Roman legal practices and dispel some of the ill will that continued to mount up between the classes. To make their rule easier and more efficient, they were also allowed for their one-year tenure to rule in absolute fashion, so that any judgment they issued could not be appealed. And there were no consuls or tribunes appointed.

The first *Decemviri* were successful, admired for their virtue and praised for their wisdom. They agreed not to mount great and intimidating shows of force, since the Romans were always on guard against anyone behaving in ways that would suggest the kings of old. The *Decemviri* agreed that one of them per day would be charged with administering the government. That man would be accompanied by twelve "lictors"—bodyguards, basically—but the rest would remain unguarded. And when they performed their assigned task, the promulgation of laws, they did so with humility: "having published Ten Tables of Law, they called the people of Rome to an assembly, urging them to go and read the laws that had been proposed . . . the hope was that the people of Rome would feel that they not only consented to accept the laws, but that they also had a part in proposing them."[10] The *Decemviri* enacted their responsibilities in an exemplary fashion, in other words, leading but also by soliciting input, earning deserved esteem and respect.

But as their one-year term was coming to an end, it was thought that the Ten Tables ("tables" means something like "tablets") were not enough and that two more would be necessary. Thus it was deemed necessary to elect another group of *Decemviri* to accomplish this task. The only member of the original *Decemviri* to want to stand for re-election was a man named Appius Claudius Crassus, a patrician who cynically ingratiated himself with the plebeians to gain their support. He was, as Machiavelli termed him in his own reading of Livy on this point, "a man shrewd and restless"—*uomo sagace e inquieto*.[11]

By hook and by crook, Appius not only had himself re-elected—a sign of excessive ambition in the eyes of some—but also engineered the election alongside him of inferior men, even as he blocked the candidacies of more qualified aspirants. And then, "It was at that very moment that Appius threw off his mask."[12] He colluded with his newly elected colleagues and schemed so that the *Decemviri* could gain absolute power. His real character having come through, other vices materialized both collective and individual. The *Decemviri* broke from the custom of having lictors present only for one man at a time, instead resorting to appearing in public as a body, with each *Decemvir* having his own twelve lictors in tow, now carrying axes as well as the traditional symbolic rods (emblems of royal power).

They now seemed a terrifying group, backed by the immediate threat of violence. The result was that both the plebeians and the senatorial class grew to fear and to hate the *Decemviri*.

The *Decemviri* did succeed in gathering together the final two Tables of law, the task that was their real *raison d'être*, but then they schemed to be re-elected: "It was clear that they aimed to have absolute rule. One mourned for liberty lost."[13] Their tyrannical ineptitude leapt from the domestic to the foreign sphere: "It was not enough that Rome's spirit was crushed, for she began to be despised by the peoples beyond her borders, who looked down on the fact that a state should possess power that had lost her liberty."[14] The ever-present threat of enemy actions—in the forms of raids on surrounding rural territory or outright war—grew daily.

Spirits were so low that it was difficult even to muster the Senate, because the patricians had mostly abandoned the city, biding time at their country estates. Eventually enough senators returned to Rome to allow debate. Though indignation and recriminations against the *Decemviri* were voiced, the senatorial class was so concerned about the rising power of the plebeians that they did not push hard enough to have the *Decemviri* disband. The necessity of establishing military commands made the *Decemviri* decide to appoint two of its members to lead in the coming struggle, one of whom was Appius, who, given his "ruthlessness, was considered more apt to crush civil disturbances."[15] What this meant was that, as military campaigns were being waged against Rome's enemies, Appius was left at home in Rome. As to the battles, the soldiers were so uninspired by the leadership, drawn from the *Decemviri*, that the Roman armies suffered notable defeats.

As to Rome itself, conditions deteriorated with Appius alone and holding power, for it so happened that he conceived an abominable lust for a young girl of "humble birth," Virginia, whose father, Lucius Virginius, "was an honorable man, who had an admirable record, both in his home life and in his military career."[16] Virginia had already been betrothed to another soldier, a plebeian and former tribune named Lucius Icilius, who was "a proven, keen champion of the people."[17] So all the ingredients were there for significant, indeed explosive, conflict, all the more so when it became clear what terrible plans Appius had in mind. What he did was to have one of his dependants, named Claudius, claim Virginia as his slave, trumping up a charge that she was not in fact the daughter of Virginius. She was compelled to appear before a judge—Appius himself, surprise—who proceeded to inform her that she, "a girl born in his house, had been taken and foisted off on Virginius as his daughter."[18] Virginia had advocates too, who pointed out that, as her father was now outside of Rome readying to fight, soldier that he was, he should at least be allowed to come back before the trial proceeded. Nevertheless, Appius, dripping with sarcasm, ruled that she should remain in custody of Claudius until her so-called father could return. Then her betrothed, Lucius Icilius, arrived on the scene and made a speech full of emotion, saying he would rather die himself than let her be turned over into Appius's hands. Appius replied that Icilius was only a populist troublemaker, stirring up unrest as these demagogic tribunes often did.

Enough time went by that Virginius, Virginia's father, was summoned back to Rome, even though Appius had tried to refuse him leave from his military detachment. But Appius returned, and "at dawn the next day the city was alive with excitement."[19] Virginius attempted to convince his fellow Romans that Appius's conduct was an outrage and that "it was for their own children and wives that they stood in the battle line every day . . . but at what price, if, though the city was safe, his children had to suffer the same crimes as if trapped in a captured city?"[20] Appius however was unmoved by Virginius's passionate oratory and from his authoritative perch ruled on the case and gave his judgment for the plaintiff (for himself, essentially). Virginia was thenceforth to be Appius's slave, and he, mindful of what the reaction might be, brought with him an armed escort to claim his property. Virginius then persuaded Appius to give permission to talk to Virginia's nurse—the woman who had had the responsibility of raising her and would know her early circumstances best (this was possible, because in antiquity children were often sent away during their early years)—and then, Virginius said, "if I find I am not her father, at least I can go away with a more peaceful heart."[21] And so, "Virginius received permission, and he led Virginia and her nurse to the shops by the Shrine of Cloacina . . . from a butcher he snatched a knife and said, 'my dear daughter, this is the only way that I can make you free.' Then he stabbed the girl in the heart, and as he looked back toward the tribunal, he said, 'you, Appius! It is on your head that the curse of this blood will rest!' "[22] The father was so distraught at his daughter's being sent into presumably sexual servitude that he deemed it best that she die, rather than face dishonor. So he stabbed his daughter to death in public.

Virginius escaped, and Virginia's erstwhile suitor, Icilius, along with his uncle "lifted the lifeless body to show to the crowd, and they lamented Appius's crime, the girl's ill-starred beauty, and the necessity of the father's deed."[23] Virginius's crime was "necessary." He made it back to his military post, where he was seen from afar, because he was escorted by "about four hundred men who accompanied him with sympathy, roused up as they were at the vileness of the affair."[24] When he explained himself to the puzzled soldiers, he said they should not hold him guilty of a crime whose real blame lay with Appius. As to his daughter, Virginius said: "When I saw that she was being taken like a slave to a brothel, she was already lost to me, and I thought it better that it should be by death rather than by dishonor."[25]

Virginius then urged the soldiers to help him oust Appius. They marched back to Rome, occupied one of Rome's hills—the Aventine—and were joined there by another group of soldiers led by Icilius, the fiancé. Eventually the soldiers persuaded the plebeians to leave Rome and, because many aristocrats were also gone, Rome seemed deserted. Those senators who remained persuaded the *Decemviri* to resign, the soldiers and plebeians came back and were allowed to elect their own representatives, and Virginius was elected "first of all."[26] Then new consuls were elected, whose "policy had a popular slant though it was not anti-aristocratic."[27] Appius was arrested, eventually killing himself when he saw clearly that there was no way he could escape with his life; and others who had been involved were also brought to justice: "Thus Virginia's ghost, more fortunate in death than in life, having gone house to house in search of satisfaction, could rest, since no one remained who had partaken of the crime."[28] Balance was restored, and, with a proper governmental system in place, the Romans were again free to wage war effectively and continue to increase their power.

Today, what stands out most about this story? Surely it is the honor killing of Virginia by her own father. After all, her fate was not even definitively determined when he decided to murder her in a hysterically masculine fashion: he manifested the usual underlying, pervasive anxiety that his own honor was linked to the notional purity of a woman, here his daughter, whom he saw primarily as property, as, effectively, the representation of a person rather than a person with individual rights of her own.

It is an open question how often things like this happened in the premodern western world, and indeed, the more that scholars have worked on the problem, the more they have had trouble finding nonliterary evidence for these sorts of honor killings. Still, the fact remains that Livy included this episode in an account that was, in his view, "true," which is to say that, whatever the exact sequence of underlying events might have been, a great change came about eventuated by the actions of Appius and Virginius. The tale was plausible, believable. Appius in other words did something that was seen as so outside the boundaries of proper conduct that it precipitated an equally unmeasured—but inherently understandable—reaction by Virginius: the murder of his own child. In Livy's narrative, this murder was not only comprehensible; it was enough to make Virginius an object of pity, first, and then of admiration, as his fellow Romans came to see him as a leader, electing him to a high office.

In this respect, Livy's world was Machiavelli's. Machiavelli discusses the *Decemviri* episode in a series of chapters in the *Discourses*, providing a lengthy narrative of the events to lead up to the conclusions he draws. When he arrives at the murder of Virginia, he simply says: "Appius stayed behind to govern the city, whence it happened that he became enamored of Virginia. Since he desired to take her by force, her father Virginius killed her in order to free her."[29] Machiavelli goes on to describe the troubles that followed in Rome, and he more or less summarizes the rest of the developments that Livy relates. It is worth reflecting on this simple statement, where Machiavelli evinces no surprise at Livy's recounting, because here what we see—again—is premodern Machiavelli. So when he goes on here and elsewhere in the *Discourses* to reflect, often brilliantly, on forms of government, always using Livy's text as a point of departure, we should keep this notion in mind.

Premodern—what does this mean? In the specific case of Appius, Virginia, and Virginius, it means that Machiavelli's attitudes toward women and gender were of a piece with his era. It is true that we are talking about hardnosed Machiavelli here, so that his laconic passing over of Virginia's murder represents no surprise and is another case, in his view, of one development spurring on others: outrage over the "necessary" murder led the Romans to rid themselves of the *Decemviri* and restore constitutional balance. But there is no evidence anywhere that he considered women as notional equals or as potential citizens with voting rights. No surprise there, of course, and it would be unwise to blame Machiavelli for not adhering to standards he could not conceive as possible. But we should also keep in mind what being premodern meant for Machiavelli more broadly. Passing over an honor killing is jarring to us today, the most obvious example of how different his world was from ours.

Yet there are other key conditions underlying Machiavelli's basic stances on the world that, while perhaps less stark than his take on women, do put him in a different light from the one in which he is normally seen. Recognizing these conditions is important in the case of the *Discourses* because, since it is in fact a work that is separate and distinct from *The Prince*, readers, especially in the realm of political science, have often assumed that it carries a different set of messages, that *The Prince* presents a theory of monarchical power and an argument for its political legitimacy, whereas the *Discourses* do the same for republicanism. But this notion that the two works are fundamentally different in aim is, at anything but the most superficial of levels, quite misleading. As different works they do have different purposes and characteristics, but in the end it was the same Machiavelli that wrote both works, and at roughly the same time at that.

Does Machiavelli talk more extensively in the *Discourses* about republics? Yes, that is the purpose of the work, as we learn from those parts of *The Prince* where he says things like "I will pass over discussing republics, since I discussed them at length elsewhere," by which he means probably what we now have as the first eighteen chapters of the *Discourses*.[30] Not only that, but Machiavelli has many positive things to say in the *Discourses* about republics. He is a Florentine, after all, and all things considered he thinks republics can foster more prosperity for more people: "It is not what is good for an individual that make cities great but what is good in common, and there is no doubt that this common good is not realized except in republics."[31] It is worth taking a deeper look at the chapter in which this sentiment appears, its context included, because doing so will allow us to see what Machiavelli is really after.

The *Discourses* are structured in three "books," with each book consisting of numerous chapters that, like those of *The Prince*, are relatively short and suitable to be shared with his close associates in the form of letters or conversations. Book 1 has to do with internal matters in ancient Rome—domestic policy, essentially—and its first eighteen chapters are different enough in character from the rest of the *Discourses* (they include wider-ranging references, both to Livy and to other sources) that they seem to be that very work on republics to which Machiavelli referred in *The Prince*. An interesting fact—there had been 142 books in Livy's *History*, and there are 142 chapters overall in Machiavelli's *Discourses*, something Machiavelli did to pay homage to Livy. The chapters take their departure from episodes in Livy, and they reflect Machiavelli's deep, repeated reading of that classic. He has the text beside him when he writes, and he often quotes Livy verbatim, many times in Latin. He oscillates, as he does in *The Prince*, between using third person and second person, so that here too the writing seems conversational rather than systematic, or abstract—as if he has an interlocutor in mind ready to challenge him, to respond, to react.

The particular chapter under discussion here is the second chapter of book 2, where Machiavelli's express intention is to discuss matters related to the ways the ancient Romans expanded their power. But he prefaces book 2 in his usual way—a little angry, a little judgmental, and certainly reflecting the conversations he was having at the time. In fact here, in book 2 overall and in this preface especially, he is very repetitive, or rather, he wants to look at the same thing from different vantage points: "Men always praise ancient times and put down the present, not always rightly."[32] They are usually wrong to do so, but there are many reasons why they may be wrong.

First, people who praise the past excessively necessarily rely on written accounts, which can be misleading both because so much is missing and because writers tend to be favorable to success, omitting much that would cast victors in a bad light. Then there may be instances where the present is superior to the past, especially if you are speaking of the lives and habits of men in the present, whom you can observe more in the round than you can those of ancient times. In addition—in a variation of a sentiment he often applies to the fundamental nature of humanity—Machiavelli judges that "the world has always been the same and has always had in it the same amount of good as of bad," which varied according to place and, eventually, according to time, as "the world" (standing in for fate, or fortune, in this instance) "placed its power first in Assyria, then in Media [the kingdom of the Medes, in what is present-day northwestern Iran], then Persia, and then finally in Italy and Rome."[33] Again, the powerful presences of change and fortune in Machiavelli's imagination make themselves apparent. Finally, Machiavelli wants to recognize a truism, which is that people always find fault with the present, since "human desires are insatiable, because nature has given them the capacity and the possibility to desire everything, but fortune has decreed that they can only attain little. The result is a never-ending lack of satisfaction in people's minds and a weariness in what they have attained."[34] So people find fault with the present, praise the past, and live in anticipation of the future, "even though they are stimulated to do so by no reasonable cause."[35]

Machiavelli has chewed over this problem—praising the past and not esteeming the present—from every possible angle. He clearly wants his reader to know that he is well aware that people do this often, that he has considered the problem thoroughly, and that he is not just wading into a discussion with unexamined assumptions guiding him. Now we get to the real point: "So I do not know whether I will deserve to be numbered among those who deceive themselves if in these *Discourses* of mine I overpraise the times of the ancient Romans and find fault with our own."[36] Point taken. Still: "And really, if the excellence that then prevailed and the corruption that prevails now were not clearer than the sun, I would go ahead and speak more cautiously, hesitating as I might to fall into the same deception of which I accuse others."[37] The difference is clear, Machiavelli goes on to say, and so he will be clear about what he intends to say, bold even, "so that young spirits who happen to read what I write will flee from present examples and imitate those of the ancients."[38] Here, again, there is a fundamental continuity with *The Prince*: Machiavelli will write to provide astute readers with examples, good and bad, to follow and to avoid, so that what he writes will be useful. He has taken a long time to get to the real point of the preface, which is to tell the reader the purpose of book 2: "Since we spoke, in the *Discourses* of the previous book, of the decisions the Romans made that pertained to domestic policies, in this one we shall speak of the decisions the Romans made that pertained to the increase of their empire."[39] In other words, book 2 will be about what to do well and what to avoid if a state wants to prosper and to increase its domain.

Why did Machiavelli take so long to arrive at the main message of the preface? To answer to this question, we need to take a look at his audience, where he was in the arc of his career and life when writing, and what point Florentine history had reached.

Who is his audience? Keep in mind that the *Discourses* represent yet another work not printed in Machiavelli's lifetime. That fact, coupled with what one of Machiavelli's contemporaries, Filippo Nerli, tells us, allows us insight into whom Machiavelli might have had in mind as he wrote. A Florentine, occasional diplomat, and eventual governor of the northern city of Modena (by commission of the later Medici pope, Clement VII), Nerli lived from 1485 to 1566 and wrote a history of Florence that covered the years 1217 to 1537. In it, he tells of an interesting moment in Florence that takes place at what we know as the "Rucellai gardens," the meeting place of a literary discussion group. And if we want to understand Machiavelli's real audience, we need to investigate the nature of this group.

The Rucellai gardens represented a sort of salon that was familiar to many Renaissance men (as well as the occasional woman, especially as the sixteenth century wore on). These groups often morphed later in the sixteenth century into more formal academies, but in Machiavelli's day they had a half-informal, half-formal flavor, as friends and acquaintances gathered at an appointed time and place to discuss a topic already agreed upon, contemplated poems or other works in progress, and heard musical or theatrical performances. The Rucellai, a prominent Florentine family, had hosted meetings like this for some time. Their crest stands on the beautiful façade of the church of Santa Maria Novella in Florence (these days near Florence's train station), designed by the polymath Leon Battista Alberti and financed by the Rucellai.

In this case, Nerli in his history discusses a conspiracy that was hatched in 1522, against Cardinal Giulio de' Medici, who would soon become Pope Clement VII.[40] Nerli writes that the conspirators would have been much the wiser and perhaps not have attempted this foolish act if they had been more familiar with Machiavelli's thoughts on the subject in his *Discourses*. (Nerli was right: in the sixth chapter of book 3 of the *Discourses*, Machiavelli delineates how difficult it can be to carry out conspiracies.)

Nerli outlines how "there had met for quite some time in the Rucellai gardens a certain group of young men of letters and of great talent . . . among whom Niccolò Machiavelli was a regular member (and I was a great friend of Niccolò's and of all of them, with whom I very often associated)." He goes on to say that this group devoted a great deal of time to studying history and above all that they had encouraged Machiavelli to compose "that book of his of *Discourses on Livy*" while Cosimo Rucellai was still alive (Cosimo Rucellai died in 1519).[41] Evidence like this, as well as other sources, allows us to date the composition of the *Discourses* to approximately the years 1513–1517, so that, after the white heat of *The Prince*, Machiavelli settled in to write the *Discourses*. It is likely that the first eighteen chapters of the *Discourses* served as a kind of pendant to *The Prince* and were written at around the same time.

But Machiavelli wrote the rest of the *Discourses* over a period of a number of years. Here again his style can be explained by the fact that he developed his ideas in conversation, in the company of others, whom he expected to challenge his ideas, in a process that then sent him back to his desk to rewrite, to revise, and to clarify his positions. So one can imagine easily—to return to Machiavelli's lengthy musings on how much to praise antiquity and to find fault with the present—that he had presented his *Discourses* in short segments to his friends at the gardens. And one can conceive that he had heard from his conversation partners that one had to be cautious, that the earlier Renaissance's unqualified praise of antiquity was not always and everywhere advisable, and that as a result one needed to take a balanced approach. Besides, as we have seen in the case of how to deal with the rebellious people of the Valdichiana, Machiavelli had experienced what happened when he included a lengthy statement about Livy in a proposal to the Florentine government. Nothing. Invoking Roman conduct unqualifiedly was not enough. Reflection was necessary, the kind of sustained reflection he was providing in his drawn-out *Discourses*.

And where was Machiavelli during this four-year period, 1513–1517? What was happening in his city? What was he doing? He comes back to his beloved city, first of all, hoping as ever to renew his career. The Medici were riding high, with Leo X in the papal chair and increasing ambitions for the family in Florence, Rome, and the rest of Italy. Leo's nephew, Lorenzo de' Medici the Younger, had been put in charge of Florence in 1513 and, three years later, was made duke of Urbino when Leo engineered the conquest of that city in the Marches. It was at that point, by the way, that Machiavelli dedicated *The Prince* to Lorenzo the Younger, still trying to melt the icy hearts of the Medici. In the meantime, Machiavelli continued his work—on Livy, to be sure, but also (most likely in 1514) finishing a version of his second *Decennale*, detailing in poetic form the ten years between 1504 and 1514, a companion piece to his first *Decennale* of 1504. And during this period Machiavelli became a regular attendee at the meetings of the Rucellai gardens, where his progress on these and other works was shared, information was exchanged, and, possibly, political matters were discussed, including how and whether to try to change Florence back into an aristocratic republic, as it had been during the Soderini years.

Perhaps the *Discourses* formed part of those political conversations. Indeed it would be hard to imagine that they did not. But more than a political program, the *Discourses* show, again, Machiavelli the observer, the protoanthropologist, and the thinker who possessed—as his friendly rival Francesco Guicciardini told him in a 1521 letter—a *contraria professione*, a "contrary profession."[42] When Guicciardini wrote that letter in 1521, he had published his own *History of Florence* and was emerging as a respected political actor in Florence. In his letter to Machiavelli, Guicciardini was referring to religion, reflecting the relatively common knowledge that Machiavelli was not, to put it mildly, a very pious man. But in the exchange of letters that followed, Machiavelli embraced the notion that he was of a "contrary profession," both in terms of religion but also in terms of the opinions of others.[43] This too is another key that allows us to unlock the *Discourses*: Machiavelli is just not like everyone else, sometimes going a bit too far, but always keeping his steely eye on practicalities. His thoughts on republics, as these manifest themselves in the *Discourses*, are not that different from those in *The Prince*, or rather, they need to be seen as part of one unitary vision.

Let us take religion, for starters. Here we find ourselves in book 1 of the *Discourses*, chapters eleven through fifteen, part of that first eighteen-chapter section written roughly at the same time as *The Prince*. From the beginning, Machiavelli tells his readers, Rome had a healthy respect for religion, one that was begun and cultivated by its second king, Numa Pompilius,

Romulus's successor. Upon taking over, Numa found a "people quite savage, and desiring to induce them to obey the laws by means of the arts of peace, turned to religion as something thoroughly necessary if he wished to maintain a state."[44]

"Maintain a state." Here Machiavelli uses the words *mantenere una civiltà*—elsewhere he will say *mantenere lo stato*. This is really the principal concern, whether in republics or princedoms: finding and maintaining order and stability in a world in which stability seems impossible to find. Religion, practiced correctly, serves as a key ingredient: "Whoever takes a good look at Roman history sees how important religion was in mobilizing the armies, firing up the people, keeping men good, and making the wicked ashamed."[45] Numa, Romulus's successor who instituted these salutary Roman religious practices, realized he needed to have religion to provide order, so he "pretended to be in contact with a nymph" from whom he drew recommendations about what to tell the Romans.[46] The Romans, believing him to be in contact with the divine, allowed Numa to carry out the desired reforms. Machiavelli's Italian verb for "pretended" is *simulò*, which does a good, classicizing job of translating Livy's original *simulat* (which Livy had used in telling the story of Numa and the notional nymph, Egeria; Machiavelli adjusts the tense of the verb). No ambiguity: Numa was pretending.

Religion is one thing, primarily: instrumental. It points toward no greater truths, though it makes people believe there are such truths, and it possesses utility only in so far as it contributes to political order. It is especially important to use religion when proposing something new politically—a new political order, a change in government, and so on.

Now it is true that it may be easiest to employ religion in this instrumental fashion with unsophisticated folk ("quite savage" as were Numa's early Roman compatriots). But it is not only unsophisticated people whom religion's motivating force can sway when introducing political novelty. After all—and here we return to the Machiavelli who, if not exactly tactless, again goes a bit too far—"The people of Florence did not believe themselves to be either ignorant or crude, but nevertheless they were persuaded by Fra Girolamo Savonarola that he spoke with God."[47] From something ancient, Machiavelli moves to something modern, to an episode he experienced up close, the presence of Girolamo Savonarola in Florence. You have the sense that he was amazed then, when it was all happening in the 1490s, and that he is still astonished at what Savonarola was able to accomplish. There is the usual rhetorical caution, barely disguising irony: "I don't want to judge whether this was true or not, since one should speak of such a man only with great reverence."[48] "But"—and by now we understand that a "but" was on the way, inevitably—"I am here to say that vast numbers of people believed him without having seen even one thing out of the ordinary to make them believe in him." Meaning, there were no miracles, there was nothing supernatural, nothing at all, really, except a man and his own unique, persuasive comportment: "his life, his learning, and the subject he chose to speak about were enough to make them have faith in him."[49]

Here as elsewhere Machiavelli's opinion about Savonarola speaks volumes. Just as in *The Prince*, when Savonarola came up in the context of Moses, Theseus, and other great leaders, Savonarola seems worthy of admiration and respect to Machiavelli, since—through whatever magic of charisma, cleverness, and political instincts—he was able to convince Florentines that his suggestions concerning governance were the best. Savonarola was a real leader, whose only major failing was that he was—as Machiavelli says in chapter six of *The Prince*—an unarmed prophet. He reached the pinnacle of power by convincing Florentines that he was speaking with God. "So let none of this make anyone fear that he cannot carry out what has been carried out by others, since men, as was said in our preface, are born and have lived and died in one and the same way."[50] Here is the key, if we are thinking about republics versus monarchies, and so on: people are always the same. They will not change their fundamental natures regardless of the form of government in which they find themselves enmeshed. And whatever form of government may exist, religion can be a powerful tool for that government's leadership if it is deployed correctly.

What Machiavelli has in mind here with his focus on the ancient Romans is relatively clear. By "religion" he means a combination of three things: large-scale ceremonies that lead to awe, rituals—which by their repetition and seasonal nature help afford people structure (thus ensuring a kind of stability)—and finally the sense thus produced that civic obligations are undergirded by something more than just the transitory world of mundane existence. If an obligation—to obey laws, say, or to serve one's country faithfully in war abroad or in peace at home—has more than just a purely secular-seeming quality, if, in other words, that obligation comes to seem more than purely contractual, then a society can cohere, evolve, and prosper. When people carry out their civic duties, they feel that they are working for something larger than themselves and, since people do want recognition for their efforts, they believe that the fulfillment of their obligations (divinely tinged as these seem) will be rewarded by public recognition both in their lifetime and after they are gone. This public recognition—glory, in other words, that individuals win for themselves in life and after death—is something to be desired not just for selfish reasons, but also for the flourishing of the state, since the state is part of a divine social economy.

And Catholicism—both the Catholic Church as an institution, but even more deeply, some of the core principles of the Catholic religion—does not fit the bill, at least as far as Machiavelli is concerned. "Because many are of the opinion that the flourishing of Italy's cities is due to the Roman Church, I want to argue against this opinion."[51] There are two main reasons, Machiavelli says. The first is that the papal court offers terrible examples of behavior, the result of which is that Italy "has lost all devotion and all religion . . . the first thing, then, that we Italians owe to the Church and to priests is that we have become irreligious and wicked."[52] Even more grave is "the second reason for our ruin: this is that the Church has held and continues to hold Italy divided."[53] Machiavelli's outburst against the morality of churchmen represents nothing new, really, as Italy had—and has—a robust tradition of anticlericalism going back to Boccaccio's ribald satires in his fourteenth-century *Decameron*. But the second point, to the effect that the church serves as a vehicle of "national" division, leads into more interesting territory.

First, Machiavelli says that the church "has held and continues to hold Italy divided." The expression translated as "Italy," in this case, is *questa provincia*—"this province," most literally. Elsewhere Machiavelli does use *Italia* to signify "Italy." But the diverse names signify something more than arbitrary linguistic choices. They reflect, instead, Italy's divided nature, whereby a Florentine was more likely to consider himself a Florentine than an Italian, unless what we see geographically as Italy was under attack from outside forces. This problem of regionalism, which continues to plague Italy today, is something that Machiavelli implicitly recognizes in much of his work, and explicitly here, when he writes in the very next sentence: "And the truth is that no *provincia* has ever been united or happy if it was not under the dominion of either a republic or a prince, as has happened in France and Spain."[54]

"Happy." Here the word Machiavelli uses is *felice*, which also means "fortunate" or "flourishing," so that we see yet again what Machiavelli is designating: the opposite of weak, divided, and unstable, the mirror image of that by which he found himself surrounded, an ideal toward which one could aim but at which one might never arrive. The reason? "Though the Church is headquartered in Italy and does have temporal power, it has been neither powerful nor virtuous enough to take power in Italy and become its leader."[55] Yet it has not been so weak that it was not able to persuade foreign powers to come in and help it maintain its temporal domains. This is why Italy has come under the sway of "so many different princes and lords, from which there has arisen such a lack of unity, such weakness, that it has become the prey, not only of foreign power, but of anyone who decides to attack it."[56]

Then, mordantly, finally, clearly: "For all of this the rest of us Italians have no one else to thank but the church."[57]

So the church is problematic in a political sense. It is, as we learned in *The Prince*, a special kind of princedom, an "ecclesiastical" princedom, with different rules from the rest of all imaginable governments. Yet there is even more food for thought here, when we note that Machiavelli mentions France and Spain. Without knowing it, he was looking toward the future, as he gestures to the next big step in the evolution of European power politics: the emergence of large, centralized, sovereign states, with Spain, the Dutch, France, and England as the models. Spain, the Dutch republic, and England would take the lead in the great, world-changing shift in trade, as trade routes moved from the Mediterranean to the Atlantic. And later, in the seventeenth and eighteenth centuries, France, with its strong center in Paris, would become the model of a centralized absolute monarchy.

For all of these things, fifteenth-century Italy had provided microcosmic models that helped embed certain traditions and tendencies in the European imagination: Florentine merchants' propensity to travel and their sophisticated banking practices conditioned people to the ideas and practices of international trade. The voyages of a certain Genoese ship captain sailing under the Spanish flag in 1492 are well known. Fifteenth-century Italian courts, like that of Federico da Montefeltro, duke of Urbino, whose craggy visage was immortalized in his portrait by Piero della Francesca, provided in their mixture of cultural sophistication and political power the seeds out of which later absolutisms grew.

But there is no other way to say it: things were getting bigger, and Italy stayed small. Machiavelli—in this subtle gesture to France and Spain—saw, dimly and in a necessarily adumbrated fashion, that if Italy did not go this route, it would be sunk, forever prey to outside forces. And, of course, he was exactly right.

It is not only the church with which Machiavelli finds fault, when it comes to religion. The problem is Christianity itself, with its exaltation of humility, its otherworldliness, its sense that life on earth represented only a transitory pilgrimage (as Saint Augustine had outlined in such a lasting fashion in his *Confessions* in the early fifth century). At one point in the *Discourses* Machiavelli wonders why Romans and other ancient peoples were more ardent "lovers of liberty," by which he means more concerned with maintaining their political independence. He goes on: "I believe this is owed to the same reason that makes men less strong, which has to do with the difference between how we are raised and how the ancients were raised, which is itself based on the difference between our religion and ancient religion."[58] We know where we are going with this: "since our religion has shown us the truth and the true way, it makes us think less of worldly honor, whereas the pagans, thinking very highly of worldly honor and indeed deeming it to be the highest good, were much more savage in their actions."[59] "The truth and the way" allude of course to the gospel of John (14.6), where Christ says, "I am the way, the truth and the light," so that Machiavelli is taking a phrase that would have resonated in his readers' minds and deploying it, once again, in a lightly ironic fashion.

"Bold versus humble" is Machiavelli's theme going forward here. Ancient religious practices were punctuated by magnificent public sacrifices, which were "full of blood and savagery, killing a multitude of animals, something that, tremendous as it was, made men similar," by which he means similarly ferocious, bold, and full of strength.[60] In addition: "Ancient religion did not divinize men unless they were themselves full of worldly glory, such as were military captains and leading men of republics. Our religion, instead, has glorified humble and contemplative men, rather than active men."[61] Machiavelli goes on to say that when Christianity demands that one be strong, the strength required is the strength to suffer (like martyrs), rather than the strength to do something bold (like vanquish a difficult enemy). Machiavelli here criticizes the Christian exaltation of saints and takes a side in a debate that had a long history: whether the active or contemplative life is better. For a society to be strong, Machiavelli clearly believes that men of action are needed. "And so, this way of life seems to have made the world weak," easy prey for the wicked, with everyone willing to suffer oppression, rather than avenge it, in the hope of making it to paradise.[62]

Then it is time for a little of the old, classic "masculine/feminine" dichotomy: "Now even if it seems as if the world has become effeminate and heaven powerless, this is certainly due to the cowardice of the men who have taken our religion to be one of inaction rather than strength. For were they to consider that religion permits us to exalt and defend our homeland, they would see that religion demands that we love and honor our homeland and that we train ourselves to be such as can defend it."[63] The implicit premise is that those who foster religion ought to see that it must be mobilized as a political force. "Lots of luck," seems to be his implicit undertone, and once again we see a Machiavelli who goes, if not too far, just right up to the edge of acceptability, implicitly and explicitly accusing religious and secular leaders of that worst of premodern flaws: being effeminate, not wielding power like men.

The rest of the *Discourses* reflect the same values we see in *The Prince*: the primacy of military power when it comes to politics, an instrumental view of religion, the fundamental notion that people are the same when it comes to their emotions. The *Discourses* represented another work unprinted in Machiavelli's lifetime, with its first printed edition only in 1531, four years after his death.

Meanwhile, as he was writing the *Discourses*, he was also working his way back into public life.

6

The Comedy of Life

LETTERS AND PLAYS, WIVES AND LOVERS

◆ ◆ ◆

"Di cosa nasce cosa"—"One thing begets another." This line appears in Machiavelli's comic play *Mandragola (The Mandrake Root)*, on which he was working alongside the *Discourses*. The title refers to a plant that was associated with fertility and appears in the Bible.[1] And the comedy shows us another side of Machiavelli, even as it allows insight into the same Machiavelli we know from his other works. Yes, alongside the hard-nosed theorist there resided a person of an essentially comic temperament. But that comic temperament emerged from Machiavelli's appreciation of chance, fortune, individuals, and misunderstanding. The play is by turns funny, scabrous, and by our standards completely—but typically for Machiavelli's era—politically incorrect.

Here is the basic story. A young Florentine man, Callimaco, has spent twenty years in France. Hearing that there is a marvelous beauty back home in Florence, he is inspired to go see her for himself. He returns, gets a look, and is inflamed with an unquenchable passion for Lucrezia, the virtuous daughter of her formerly not so virtuous mother, Sostrata. Callimaco simply must have her: "I am on fire with such a great desire to see her that I can find no peace."[2] The problem is that she is already married, as it happens, to a rather slow, grumpy lawyer, who is much older than she, named Messer Nicia ("Messer" was an honorific title used to indicate that the person so called had a certain status in Florence—not noble, but very respectable).

Messer Nicia is having problems of his own, since, despite trying, he and Lucrezia have not been able to have a child. A former matchmaker whom Callimaco has befriended, and with whom poor old Nicia was close, has convinced Nicia to take Lucrezia to the baths, in the hope of helping their fertility problem. Callimaco decides to meet them there, he tells his friend Ligurio, since after all *di cosa nasce cosa*—"one things begets another" and *il tempo lo governa*—"time is the master." But then Callimaco comes up with an even better plan, with Ligurio's aid: Callimaco will pretend to be a doctor with expertise in fertility, since Nicia is so slow that by speaking a few words of Latin to him, Callimaco believes he can pass himself off as a doctor. It works, and the following scheme is set in motion, agreed to by Nicia and helped along by Lucrezia's mother: Lucrezia will take a special potion. The first man with whom she makes love after taking the potion—so "doctor" Callimaco tells Nicia—will die. But thereafter she will be fertile, and they will conceive a child. Nicia simply must agree to this one-time cuckolding (and to sending a dupe in to make love to his wife, a dupe who will die, he believes), and then all will be well. Of course Callimaco, having concocted this story, is planning to be the man himself, in disguise. He, Ligurio, and—surprise—a corruptible friar, Fra Timoteo, Lucrezia's confessor, hatch an elaborate scheme of mutual disguises, even as Fra Timoteo and Lucrezia's mother work to persuade her that there is nothing wrong with her following this plan. Meanwhile Ligurio tells Callimaco what he must do should he finally make it into her bedroom: "Explain the trick to her, show her the love you bring her, tell her how much you love her and how she can be your lover with no dishonor and how she can be your enemy, but with a great loss of her honor. Once she spends the night with you, she won't want it to be the last."[3]

The long and the short of it is that this is exactly how matters play themselves out. Callimaco (we learn in his postlovemaking recounting to Ligurio) promises Lucrezia that, should she accept him, he will be her most devoted lover and marry her after the aged Nicia dies. Lucrezia—"once she had thought about my arguments and about how different it was to make love with me versus Nicia and between the kisses of a young lover and an old man"—agrees.[4] She accepts Callimaco, urges him to come to church with her and Nicia that day and thereafter to dine with them, thence to become a close family friend. Nicia, believing Callimaco to be a doctor who had helped solve his problem, is none the wiser. When they do meet, believing this is the first meeting between "doctor" Callimaco and Lucrezia, old Nicia says, "Doctor, give my wife your hand," in other words, "shake my wife's hand" but obviously—to the audience if not to Nicia—also a sly play on what has happened between them.[5] The play ends with the friar wishing the audience well. The beautiful young Lucrezia, needless to say, is a device, not a person, who has no voice of her own. We learn of her conduct and of the way she accepted Callimaco's trickery only through his recounting.

Di cosa nasce cosa. This is probably an opportune time to digress and to mention that there is a manuscript in the Vatican

Library that possesses two interesting features.[6] First, it contains copies of two ancient Latin texts: Lucretius's *On the Nature of Things* and Terence's *Eunuch*. Second, the entire manuscript is written in Machiavelli's hand and was copied by him sometime before 1498. Why is this relevant? First, there is Lucretius (who died around 50 BC). *On the Nature of Things* is his only known work, a complete version of which was lost to the Middle Ages.[7] When the Florentine humanist Poggio Bracciolini rediscovered it while attending the Council of Constance in 1417, it caused a stir for a number of reasons.

On the Nature of Things, like many other ancient texts that came to the attention of fifteenth-century thinkers, was something from the ancient world that they loved so well but was nonetheless "new," meaning it was known to have existed but had not been read extensively in the Middle Ages, since a full version of the text was not known. So like other ancient pagan texts, Lucretius's *On the Nature of Things* was important to Renaissance thinkers who were eager to learn ever more about the ancient world. And it didn't hurt—to an age in search of models of how to write—that Lucretius wrote hauntingly beautiful Latin. But Lucretius was different, for he was the main Latin transmitter of ancient Epicureanism, a philosophy noteworthy for advocating both atomism and the pleasure principle. As to the pleasure principle, it is less radical than it sounds. Human beings should pursue pleasure, since it is a natural inclination. "Pleasure" means having one's desires satisfied. So, if through spiritual exercise an individual is able to reduce his desires, he thus can experience more pleasure. In this respect Epicureanism was like other Hellenistic schools of philosophy (including Stoicism and Skepticism) that emphasized individual development through self-control. Epicureans advocated withdrawal from politics, something that didn't sit well with a certain strain of Renaissance thought that privileged the life of political action. Nonetheless, it was another brick that Renaissance thinkers used to reconstruct the lost edifice of ancient thought.

Atomism represented something potentially more dangerous, since Lucretius's atomism was tied up with his view of God and Providence, which was simply this: while there may have been a god, this god had no interest in human affairs. All things were composed of atoms, which mix together, combine to turn into specific things—like human beings—but then when those things reach their natural end, the constituent atoms disperse again, only to recombine into other things: *di cosa nasce cosa*, in other words. Now for your basic rock, tree, or even everyday animal, all this is fine—another arrow that Renaissance thinkers could add to their quiver of theories about how the natural world worked. But when it comes to human beings, Lucretius couldn't be clearer that they, too, were part of the natural order and subject to the same dispersal after death, that there was no immortal human soul, and that even the human being, once passed from this earth, would be reduced to atoms that "move without pattern through the void."[8] This type of pure materialism meant that a central pillar of Christianity—an immortal human soul that would reap the rewards of its possessor's earthly conduct after death—would crumble. Also, the Lucretian view of divinity precluded the Christian idea of a personal god interested in individual human beings. Dilemmas.

We should not read too much into Machiavelli's throwaway line, *di cosa nasce cosa*. He is after all expressing the sentiment of a young man—his character, Callimaco—aflame with love who is willing to trust his improvisational instincts and youthful vigor to be with the object of his desire. And we should not lean too exclusively on the Lucretian dilemmas and their eventual resolution when looking at, or explaining, the Renaissance. Lucretius represented one strand—an important one, no doubt—of the sorts of dilemmas Renaissance thinkers routinely faced as they integrated their findings about the ancient world into their own views of culture. There were hundreds of ancient texts unknown to the Middle Ages that came to light in the fifteenth century: texts from the third century that seemed to recognize something like sacraments—written by notorious anti-Christians, like that of the little-known later Platonist Iamblichus.[9] How to explain this and integrate it into a Christian context? Dilemma. There were the texts of Plato himself, which were fully recovered and translated into Latin only in the fifteenth century. How to explain it when in *The Republic* he seems to advocate communism of wives and children? Dilemma. How to understand Plato's obvious references to and endorsements of homosexual conduct in some dialogues in a Christian society that officially frowned on it? Dilemma. These and many other dilemmas spurred interest, engendered creative solutions, and served as the basis for countless debates. No one author, however important, can explain major shifts in a culture's direction. But Lucretius was there in Machiavelli's reading, the object of such interest that he copied *On the Nature of Things* by hand.

There is one adjective that one would not, in the normal course of things, apply to Lucretius: funny. On the one hand Machiavelli's vision brings into relief unpredictability, the mysteries of fortune, and even the power of individual personalities and the inapplicability of transcendental values in the everyday conduct of human affairs. On the other, it is helpful to recall that many of these qualities can be found in comedy as well. In many ways, Machiavelli's sensibility is essentially comic, drawn from the things he has seen and lived, and from their seemingly random quality. One minute, a condottiere like Cesare Borgia seems to be on the verge of uniting Italy. The next, his plans fall apart because his most important patron—his father, the pope—has died. One minute, a Dominican who had people believing he spoke directly to God is in control of Florence. The next, he and his regime are up in flames. One minute, you are an important Florentine diplomat. The next, you are being tortured in a jail cell. Machiavelli did not need Lucretius to tell him the world was unpredictable. So it is equally suggestive that Machiavelli took the time to copy Terence's *Eunuch* in that very same manuscript.

Terence, the ancient comic playwright who came from North Africa and was active in the first half of the second century BC, was prized in the Renaissance, as he had been in the Middle Ages. If most ancient Latin texts were written in a deliberately "high" register, Terence by contrast wrote the way people spoke, so that Renaissance thinkers, always on the alert for ancient Latin's different registers, were intrigued. Plus, he was funny, at least by the politically incorrect standards of the premodern western world. This play, the *Eunuch*, was Terence's Latin version of a Greek play written by Menander (a comic writer active in the late fourth and early third centuries BC, very little of whose work survived). Terence's *Eunuch* has a convoluted plot, an ensemble of characters that include two young men driven almost mad by love, courtesans, witty slaves, disguised identities, and—as in Machiavelli's later *Mandragola*—an unwanted act of sexual intercourse that eventually turns into a permanent coupling. So this too was something Machiavelli saw fit to write out by hand. While the standards of what was appropriate subject matter for comedy were vastly different from those of today, Machiavelli's interest in both reading and writing comedy evinces his passion for what we might call the "comedy of life," with all of its unpredictability, fortuitous encounters, and diverse human motivations gleefully included.

Mandragola can also help us enter Machiavelli's life and social world in ways that other sources cannot do. To begin, take the case of the main character, Callimaco. We learn at the outset that he had been away from Florence for twenty years, in France. Why? Here is what Callimaco tells us: "I was ten years old when those who were responsible for me sent me to Paris, since my father and mother were dead. There I remained for twenty years. Then ten years ago, when because of King Charles's descent the wars began in Italy that are ruining this country, I made up my mind to stay in Paris and not come back to my homeland, since it seemed to me I could live safer there than here."[10] We learn first of all then that Machiavelli is setting the action of the play in 1504 (ten years after the calamitous French invasion), and that Callimaco is thirty years old. The death of Callimaco's parents might have been unusual, but a young boy from Florence's elite merchant class being sent away for a number of years was not. Often a boy was sent to another city at a young age, for two reasons: first, to learn another language, which included sometimes other varieties of Italian; second, to learn another currency system (the young Giovanni Boccaccio in the fourteenth century was sent to Naples, for example). Callimaco thus would have appeared as a typical figure to the audience Machiavelli was trying to reach. At the age of thirty, too, Callimaco would have been expected to enter into an arranged marriage with a woman of much younger age, in her mid to late teens. Callimaco also shows all the signs of a youth mad with passion, a stock figure in ancient as well as in Renaissance literature and one of the main reasons arranged marriages were thought desirable. Marriage existed, in Machiavelli's era (indeed well into modern times), to pass on property, to bear children, and to ally families who desired to be linked for social or political reasons. Romantic love was not the point.

Machiavelli himself married a young woman, Marietta Corsini, in 1501. He was thirty-two years old, right on schedule. Like most married women of the time, Marietta was usually pregnant or nursing during her child-bearing years, and despite having lost several children (typical losses in Machiavelli's day), she and Niccolò had five who lived: a daughter, Bartolomea, and four sons, named Bernardo, Ludovico, Piero, and Guido.

We have one poignant letter from Marietta to Machiavelli from 1503, about two years after they were married (and soon after the birth of their second child). Machiavelli is in Rome, where there was an outbreak of plague at the time:

> My dearest Niccolò. You make fun of me, but you are wrong to do so, since I would be doing much better if you were here. You know very well how happy I am when I know you are not down there, and especially now that I hear there is great disease down there. . . . Please send me letters a little more often than you do,

since I have had only three of them. . . . For now the baby is doing well, he looks like you: he is as white as the snow, but his head looks like black velvet, and he is hairy like you. Because he looks like you, he is beautiful to me. He seems to have been in the world for a year already: he opened his eyes as soon as he was born and he started making noise all through the house. But our daughter is not feeling that well. Remember to come home. That's all. May God be with you and protect you. I am sending you a doublet, two shirts, two kerchiefs, and a towel that I am sewing for you. Your Marietta, in Florence.[11]

No reply has survived from Niccolò. A few days later, Machiavelli got a letter from a friend saying about Marietta: "God knows it's impossible to get her to calm down and relax."[12]

Overall, there are a number of letters in Machiavelli's sizeable correspondence in which Marietta is mentioned. They reveal a young wife doing her duty according to the standards of the time—bearing children—but who also greatly missed her husband when he was away. One of his correspondents, Biagio Buonaccorsi, wrote Machiavelli repeatedly while the Florentine secretary was in Rome in this early period, giving him news on everything from the progress of some tailoring Machiavelli wanted done to news of his wife both before and after the birth of his son. The letters are coarsely funny, and they reflect the tone in which the friends talked to each other. Vulgar, quick wit was coin of the realm, so some of the more extreme-sounding sentiments should not be taken at face value. For example, on December 21, 1502, Biagio writes to Machiavelli: "Madonna

Marietta curses God and talks as if she has thrown away her body and her possessions. Please, for your own sake, arrange it so that she gets her dowry like other women."[13] Or on the following day: "To Niccolò Machiavelli, his honored brother. Stick it up your ass, since we're sending you money, cloth and everything you're asking for, and Madonna Marietta is desperate."[14]

Then on November 2, 1503, as the birth of the baby was approaching: "Marietta hasn't given birth yet, and if my little boy weren't very sick (and hasn't yet raised his head from the pillow), I would have sent my wife over to her."[15] Then the baby is born, as we learn from a letter of another of Machiavelli's friends, named Luca Ugolini: "Congratulations! Really, your dear Madonna Marietta did not deceive you, since he is your spitting image. Leonardo da Vinci wouldn't have done a better portrait."[16] Then Biagio weighs in again, on November 15: "We'll see to it that your little sprout will make you proud, don't worry. But he looks like a little crow, he is so dark."[17] And so it goes: Machiavelli's friends tease and kid him while he is away, which is often. They share the assumption, so important that it did not need to be stated, that children represented the real cementing of a family and that no letter should go by without news of them, especially when they were in their infancy and at risk, as all babies were, of catastrophic illness. And they tell him, half-jokingly, half-seriously, that his wife "is very emotional about your absence," even as she and Machiavelli's kin were making provisions for the child.[18]

The comedy of life. We can see from Machiavelli's lack of preserved epistolary responses that his love for his wife Marietta was not the mad passion to which Callimaco was subject.

He certainly wrote her letters during his many absences, though these have not been preserved. Much later in life, as he was close to his dying days, he mentioned her with affection in a letter to his son, Guido. Machiavelli was writing from Imola, where he was once again on a diplomatic mission (having by then recovered enough political status in Florence): "Say hello to dear Madonna Marietta for me, and tell her I have been just about to leave from here for days and am expecting to do so soon. And tell her that I have never wanted to be back in Florence as much as I do now, but that there is nothing else I can do. Just tell her that whatever she hears, she should be of good cheer, since I'll be back before anything dangerous happens."[19] His affection for his wife was quiet, born of the regular familiarity that many years together engender.

Did Machiavelli ever feel Callimaco's mad passion? Yes indeed. The truth is that Machiavelli was always prone to falling in love. And like many men then and now, he was willing to pay for the privilege. Two names of "respectable courtesans" come up repeatedly, a woman called "La Riccia" ("Riccia" means "curly" in Italian and refers to her curly hair) and another named Barbera Salutati. The references in the letters are fleeting and allusive, usually, indicating that part of the currency of social exchange among Machiavelli and his friends included locker-room style gossip about courtesans: "Your last latter from Lyons arrived, and I have waited to answer it until you got to Florence, where I think that, thanks first to God and then to Jeanne [Machiavelli's courtesan in France], you have made it safely, and upon arriving there you may have seen La Riccia again."[20] In a December 1513 letter to his friend Francesco Vettori, Machiavelli tells of a Franciscan preacher who came to Florence and who "claims to be a prophet to get more credit as a preacher." The preacher was predicting all sorts of doom for Florence—it would go up in flames, be sacked, suffer pestilence, two million devils have been unleashed to make all this happen, and so on. The usual. Machiavelli writes: "These things got me so down yesterday that even though I was supposed to go see La Riccia, I didn't go . . . I didn't hear the sermon, since I don't observe such practices, but I have heard it talked about in this way by all of Florence."[21]

To be clear, the vast majority of what we have of Machiavelli's correspondence concerns political affairs, the normal Renaissance social business of recommending personal friends and colleagues for positions, and so on. Part of the reason for this is that Machiavelli's grandson, Giuliano de' Ricci, who edited the letters, deliberately left out of the collection things relating to "loves" and "pleasures" (*innamoramenti* and *piacevolezze*) and included only letters that, in his view, touched on "states and matters of importance" (*stati e maneggi d'importanza*).[22] But mostly it was because sex for Machiavelli and his cohort was important but secondary, seen as a natural outlet and not something about which one should agonize. Machiavelli himself sums up the attitude well in the continued exchange of letters with Vettori.[23] (By way of parenthesis, it is interesting to note that we are in the chronological universe of the composition of *The Prince*, which plays a barely noticeable role in the letters, though every mention of that masterwork as it evolved is nonetheless intriguing.)

Vettori, based in Rome and among other things getting used to the requirements that life as an ambassador imposes, writes Machiavelli on December 24, 1513. He begins by complaining that his Florentine colleagues in the orbit of the embassy, especially a certain Filippo, have been difficult about some of his behavior. "You know that I like to enjoy myself with women a bit . . . you also know that Filippo's disposition is against them. Before he came here, because where I live is a bit out of the way, some courtesans used to come visit, to see the church and the garden that are attached to my house."[24] The upshot is that Filippo disapproved, and began to mention to Vettori that these sorts of visits were unbecoming. But before Filippo could get even a few words out, Vettori says, "Since I knew what he was going to say, I interrupted him to say I understood just from those few words and that I didn't want to justify myself or hear his criticism, since up to now I had lived free and without regard, and I wanted to continue to do so as long as I had left to live. The result was that, even though he didn't really want to, he allowed women to come as they pleased."[25] Then another colleague, Giuliano, objected to the repeated visits of a mutual friend of a man named Ser Sano, who was visiting Vettori regularly on a matter related to a legal issue in which Vettori had an interest. "Giuliano, when he saw him come once, and twice, and three times, started telling me that Ser Sano is a degenerate and that . . . he was asked by certain merchants of 'good reputation' what sort of relations I had with Ser Sano, and that I should avoid relations of that sort."[26]

So much for the sexuality, to which we will return, but before that, remember that parenthesis regarding the presence of *The Prince* in these letters: "You write, and Filippo has mentioned this as well, that you have written a certain work about states. If you send it to me, I will be very grateful, and as soon as I have seen it . . . I will tell you my opinion about whether to present it to Magnificent Giuliano [de' Medici, duke of Nemours and the person to whom *the Prince* was originally to be dedicated]."[27] Machiavelli had asked Vettori to be on the lookout for positions available in Rome, but Vettori replied: "we have been looking into it, and here in Rome we don't find anything suitable."[28] Some say Giuliano may be made a legate to France, in which case Vettori will make further inquiries, but for now, things stand as they are. And again: "Once you send me that treatise, I will tell you if it seems like a good idea to come and present it."[29] Machiavelli's job search and the drama of the composition and initial murmurings about *The Prince* elicit attention and cry out to be noticed, needless to say. Machiavelli's eagerness to use his skills as a writer and a canny diplomat in order to get back into the game, Vettori's civility to Machiavelli in the face of what were obviously delicate circumstances, as he made an effort on Machiavelli's behalf but refused to get his hopes up unduly: these and many other factors make these letters come alive for anyone wanting to trace Machiavelli's career and his views on "states and matters of importance."

But here (to close that parenthesis), when we are discussing the comedy of life, the two instances that Vettori perceives as prudishness call out for comment. First, there is his desire to continue to live freely when it comes to his relations with women, as he has always done. When Vettori says, "You know that I like to enjoy myself with women a bit," for "women" he uses the term *femmine*, which connoted "less than respectable" women (it is the same term that Machiavelli uses in *Mandragola* for Sostrata, pure Lucrezia's not-so-pure mother). Partly, Vettori's statements reflect the concerns of someone in an ambassadorial position, wrestling with the potential inappropriateness of conduct that, for him, used to be routine. However, they also point to the attitude toward sex that Machiavelli and his friends maintained. The second instance sheds even more light, since it touches on homosexuality. Vettori takes it as a matter of course that there is no worry in associating with someone whose homosexual proclivities were open knowledge, and he is offended that his priggish colleague brings this up. We know from other letters that Machiavelli and Vettori included in their circle grown men who were known to have a fondness for sex with young men. It is equally obvious, too, that they both make it clear in their letters that their own preference at this age was for women. They are constructing their identities in their letters, choosing to include the personal details they consider relevant.

Machiavelli helps us understand what was going on. First, there is his reply to Vettori's letter. There, among other things, Machiavelli laments that Vettori's colleague did not understand that these visits represented "arrangements appropriate for an ambassador who, because he is bound by numerous constraints, needs some pleasure and diversion."[30] Critics are too small-minded to understand the world, they don't realize "that anyone who is considered wise by day will never be considered crazy by night, and that for anyone esteemed a decent and able man, whatever he does to refresh his soul and live happily will earn him honor rather than blame, and that instead of being called a bugger or a whore-monger he will be said to be broad-minded, cordial, and a good companion."[31] In other words, do what you want in your personal life, provided you exercise your responsibilities of office effectively. As to homosexual activity, it was officially frowned on, but considered part of growing up and even as part of a varied menu of sexual activity.

Later, the tables turned a bit, when in 1523 Machiavelli was concerned that one of his own sons, Ludovico, was engaged in a homosexual affair with another youth. Vettori writes (tellingly, perhaps, in Latin, rather than in Tuscan, which the two routinely used with each other): "Since we are verging on old age, we might be severe and overly scrupulous, and we do not remember what we did as adolescents. So Ludovico has a boy with him, with whom he amuses himself, jests, takes walks, growls in his ear, goes to bed together. What then? Even in these things perhaps there is nothing bad."[32] Florence had established a special court to prosecute certain kinds of homosexual activity, but among youth especially, it was considered almost a rite of passage.[33]

Sex, love, youth. Another letter exchange between Vettori and Machiavelli gives us some, though not many, more details about how these discussions between them went. Vettori writes Machiavelli in January 1514, complaining about being attracted to a beautiful woman: "I have become almost a prisoner of this Costanza. First one woman would come, then another"— Vettori again means courtesans here—"and I didn't have any real affection for them. Still, I had some nice times with them. And then this one came along, and I would daresay you have never seen with your own eyes a woman more beautiful or graceful . . . I can't think of anything besides her. And since I have seen you fall in love once or twice and have understood how much you suffered, I am trying to resist as best I can."[34]

Oh, and by the way: "I have seen the chapters of your work"— these would be of *The Prince*—"and I like them beyond measure, but since I don't have the whole thing, I don't want to make definitive judgment."[35] This little statement is a courtesy, of course, as if to say, "I got the chapters you sent, and they're looking good, but I haven't really got into them yet," so that he could acknowledge receipt of Machiavelli's earliest drafts of *The Prince*. How eagerly was Machiavelli awaiting a response about his embryonic masterpiece? We do not know.

But back to love. Responding to Vettori, Machiavelli says, "remembering what Love's arrows have done to me, I have to tell you how I have handled myself with him. In truth I have let him do what he wants, and I have followed him through valleys and forests, to the edges of cliffs and to the countryside."[36] Machiavelli's advice to Vettori: enjoy, "take off the saddle packs, let the bridle go, close your eyes and say, 'Go on, Love, lead me, be my master, if things work out, you will take the credit, if not, you get the blame, I am your slave."[37] A subsequent response indicates that Vettori did just that, despite his worries about his age (forty), his status (married with children, and thus desirous of saving money for them). The girl's mother brought her over, talked about terms and left Vettori alone with the girl. Then, "I couldn't help talking with her, touching her hands, her neck, and she was so beautiful and so lovely that all my resolve left me and I decided to surrender."[38] In the end, the two sophisticated men of the world just could not resist telling each other about their love affairs.

It is worth reflecting on Machiavelli and on relations between men and women. It would be untrue to say that Machiavelli's world was one of total gender separation. But it would not be far from true. For him, Vettori, and for most of his correspondents, women were seen as existing for reproduction, for the maintenance of family, and for fun. In the normal course of everyday life in Florence, say, respectable merchants, men, would spend time together out of the house in taverns after their main meal, whereas women would spend time together in their homes. This is not news, needless to say, and there are many parts of the world, even close to home, where something like this pattern still exists. Now, emphasizing this sort of patterned separation obviously misses all the unrecorded moments between men and women that transpire between family members in a home—moments of tenderness, arguments, and intimacies. Not only that, but scholars who have studied women's lives in the later Renaissance have revealed that women in some regions could initiate their own divorce proceedings and keep control of their dowries.[39] There are countless instances of women running their husbands' shops when husbands were away. And so on. In other words, women in the Renaissance often had more power over their lives than an older tradition of history writing might have assumed.

That said, in Machiavelli's day, in contrast to our own in the west, women were only very rarely put in a position to make political and military decisions. On the one hand, in Florence, children of both genders (of a certain social class) were educated together in basic arithmetic and basic literacy in the vernacular. On the other, Latin education, the basis for moving into the sorts of roles we see Machiavelli and his friends occupying, was more or less only for men (with a number of notable individual exceptions for women of the highest socioeconomic strata).

But as Machiavelli was writing there occurred a shift in Italy to the vernacular for creative works of literature and philosophy, with Machiavelli himself as one of the prime movers. Correspondingly, there was a notable rise in women authors and literary collaborators in Italy, some of whom represented precisely the sort of learned courtesan with whom Machiavelli associated.[40]

Such was Barbera Salutati, the other name that comes up—in addition to La Riccia—in Machiavelli's life as one of his love objects. She was a singer, first and foremost, and Machiavelli, at the age of around fifty-six, fell hopelessly in love with her. "Courtesan" is of course a fraught word, these days evoking primarily the sexual component of what courtesans represented in the Renaissance. But the word in Italian, *cortegiana*, is simply the feminine version of the word *cortegiano*, which we usually translate as "courtier."

Even in the Renaissance, however, the two words came to mean different things. In 1528 Baldassare Castiglione published what became a very famous book, *The Book of the Courtier (Il libro del Cortegiano)*. In it he presented a series of sprightly dialogues taking place over a few days. Set dramatically in the very early sixteenth century, the action took place at an idealized version of the court of Urbino, where Castiglione had spent time when young and of which he had rosy memories. Discussions touched on how a courtier should behave and what his ideal qualities should be. He should be well educated and well mannered, familiar with the military arts but not boorish, conversant on a wide range of topics from literature to the arts, musically inclined, and, above all, possess this one quality: *sprezzatura*. This word is notoriously difficult to define, but it basically meant "being cool," in our own vernacular, and doing so in an apparently effortless way. Possessing *sprezzatura* meant that one had all the above-listed qualities in the right measure and, importantly, that one was seen as having them in public situations. It is noteworthy that the two interlocutors who preside over the conversations are women: Elisabetta Gonzaga, the wife of the invalid ruler, Guidobaldo, and her sister in law, Emilia Pia. They are the arbiters of the topics to be discussed, on which the men in the dialogue discourse at greater length. They are learned and witty, and their presence, even in a fictive dialogue, shows that literate women could plausibly be seen as conversation partners equal in this one respect at least to men. However, Elisabetta and Emilia Pia had the advantages that accrued to nobility. Castiglione is careful, too, never to call them "courtesans"—*cortegiane*. They, and women like them, are *donne del palazzo*—"palace ladies."

But what of a woman who might not have been of noble birth but who wanted to pursue literature, or acting, or singing, or indeed any of the arts? One option was to go the route of the courtesan. For unlike today, when performers are lionized and indeed celebrity has taken on a kind of divine status, in Machiavelli's era performers of all sorts were seen as mere entertainers for those who could afford to pay. It is in this sense that we should see Barbera Salutati, with whom the aging Machiavelli developed an intense romantic fascination: she was a person who wanted to perform, a singer who gained repute, and a woman who wanted control over her life and for whom other avenues may not have been open. We know that she had her portrait painted by a then well-known Renaissance painter named Domenico Puligo, a short biography of whom was included in Giorgio Vasari's late sixteenth-century *Lives* of eminent artists, an invaluable source for Renaissance art. Vasari

says that Puligo "did a portrait of Barbara the Florentine ['*Barbara fiorentina*' as she was known], a most beautiful courtesan
and quite well known in that era, who was very beloved by many,
no less for her beauty than for her cultivated manners and especially for being a most excellent musician who sang divinely."[41]
Machiavelli met her, it seems, in 1524, and she appears in his
correspondence sporadically over the next two years.

A letter of August 7, 1525, gives a sense of how she was perceived. Machiavelli had developed a warm friendship with Francesco Guicciardini, a prominent Florentine who during these
years was in service to the papacy (as were other Florentines
during the pontificate of Clement VII, a Medici). He and Machiavelli developed an instant rapport after meeting personally
in 1522, and they initiated a lively correspondence (it was Guicciardini who had mentioned how well known Machiavelli's
"contrary profession" was).

This particular letter sees Guicciardini responding to
Machiavelli, who had done Guicciardini a favor by checking out
two properties in which Guicciardini was interested. Machiavelli had judged one of them favorable, the other, called "Fino-
chietto," not so much. So Guicciardini wrote his letter to
Machiavelli in the (female) persona of the property, calling himself "Milady Property of Finocchieto" and adopting the tone
of a well-bred, slightly offended woman, a woman who clearly
wants to distinguish herself from the company Machiavelli
sometimes keeps: "You are accustomed to your Barbera, who
tried, as do all of her kind, to be liked by everyone and, indeed, to seem, rather than to be."[42] Machiavelli should know
that there are different sorts of women, who are not only to be
judged by appearance. "But if through long experience with

these sorts of women—and I have come to understand you have never lived otherwise—you have adopted such bad habits that their immoralities seem to you good and worthy of women of our status, even still you should have kept in mind that it was rash to make a snap judgment, and that things must be judged not by their superficial aspects but rather by their substance."[43] It is a little convoluted, but what Guicciardini is saying is that Machiavelli made too harsh a judgment on this property originally, failing to see the potential it would have if it were developed properly, so that its true inner nature—rather than its initial outward appearance—would be able to shine through. Guicciardini knows Machiavelli well enough to tease him about his Barbera: she tries to please everyone, is concerned about appearances. Machiavelli, "you have never lived otherwise."

In later letters Machiavelli gives Guicciardini updates about many things, including Barbera and his preparations for a play in which she will have a role: "While you are hard at work over there, here we are not sleeping, since during these last evenings Ludovico Alamanni and I have been dining together with Barbera, and we have been talking about the play. The result is that she has offered to come with her singers to be the chorus between the acts."[44] The play in question—to come full circle—was *Mandragola*, and it was then, a few years after its original composition, that Machiavelli composed songs to be performed between the acts. For Barbera, of course. For the comedy of life.

As time went by, passionate Machiavelli kept hearing these teasing mentions of his beloved from his friends. With characteristic self-mockery, he wrote another theater piece, called *Clizia*, an updating for his own day of *Casina*, which had been written by ancient Rome's other great comic playwright,

Plautus, who alongside Terence supplied the Renaissance with models of how to write theatrical comedy. Machiavelli's play was commissioned by a wealthy, though not aristocratic, Florentine named Falconetti, who had been exiled for five years and wanted to stage a great event to celebrate his return. Its subject? An old man who falls foolishly in love. It has the usual mistaken identities, convoluted plots, and stock characters. The action culminates with the old man, Nicomaco (no accident that his name, "Nicomaco," evoked Machiavelli's own, "Niccolò Machiavelli") hatching a plot to sneak into the bed of the object of his desire, Clizia, who as it happened was to be married to Pirro, a younger man. Others who wanted to thwart the plan (not least his wife and son) contrived to have a strong male servant of the family, named Siro, in the bed instead of Clizia. Nicomaco relates what happened in the darkened room: "I took off my clothes. . . . As new husbands do, I tried to put my hands on her breast, but she took my hand in hers and didn't let me. I tried to kiss her but with her other hand she pushed my face away. I tried to get on top of her but she kicked me with her knee and practically broke my rib."[45] Nicomaco goes on to say that he then tried to persuade "her" with sweet lover's words, again to no avail, whereupon he resorted to threats, which, again, also didn't work. He gave up, finally, and went to sleep next to his bedmate in the hope that he might get lucky in the morning.

But then: "after a while I began to doze and to feel myself being poked right under my tailbone, with five or six cursed blows. I woke right up and before I got out of bed I put my hand under the sheets and found something pointy and hard."[46] A light was brought in, and instead of Clizia, "we saw

Siro, my servant, lying on the bed totally naked," who proceeded to tease and to laugh at old Nicomaco.[47] Soon thereafter, Nicomaco realizes the folly of his ways. He was defeated in love but brought to his senses, so the message of the play goes. Order was restored.

This is what comedies do: they reinforce social norms precisely by subverting them. They offer a mirror by which viewers and readers can recognize themselves as they observe exaggerated versions of recognizable characters. And, ultimately, comedies restore order.

Importantly, however, comedies make people laugh. This latter point, what engenders laughter at any given moment in history, is always and everywhere subject to context. Take a look these days at any number of comedic films from the 1940s, and, alongside hilarious slapstick, you will often find racial stereotypes that are cringe-worthy today. Comedies exist in the realm of the vernacular, of everyday speech and everyday situations: they are funny when they are funny because they tap into currently available prejudices, blind spots, and language. Machiavelli's comedies are full of double-entendres, uses of Tuscan dialect that made sense locally and in the era in which they were performed (since dialects change according to region and time). And of course they are full of scenes that were obviously funny at the time but are mortifying today.

Sometimes, comedies allow us some insight into the rest of an author's work, when the author wrote other things. Callimaco's bold, amoral scheme in *Mandragola*, for example, reminds us of Machiavelli's famous chapter twenty-five in *The Prince*, on fortune which, we remember, is "like a woman" and "favors young men" who are bolder and more inclined to take risks than old men. Callimaco's plan to win Lucrezia is bold and risky. And he clearly represents a "type" for Machiavelli: the young, savvy go-getter who schemes for and gets what he wants. By the same token, Nicomaco, the old man in *Clizia*, has advanced beyond the stage where these sorts of bold actions are even possible, let alone advisable. Instead of perpetrating a successful scheme, he has one pulled over on him, with that worst of premodern sexual consequences for a male wanting to preserve his masculinity: being on the passive end of homosexual sex. The comedy of life in plays and in letters: for Machiavelli—as for us all—it was rooted in time and place.

As Machiavelli aged, he never lost his taste for comedy, and he certainly practiced it well, since he was sought after as a comic writer. Still, he would have been the first to say that his comedies held far less importance than his historical and political work. For us, his bawdy letters, his friends' knowing replies, and his farcical plays tell us about the world in which he lived day to day: how he and his cohort related to women, what they considered amusing, how they spent their off hours. But there emerged more serious matters to which Machiavelli needed to attend. The years after 1520 saw him publish the one and only historical or political work that was printed during his lifetime, the *Art of War*. These were also the years of his last major work, his historical masterpiece, the *Florentine Histories*.

7

History

• • •

"I won't ever depart from my Romans in any example of anything. If one were to consider the way they lived their lives and
how they ordered that Republic, one would find many things
therein that would not be impossible to introduce into a society in which there remained even a speck of something good."[1]
Fabrizio, a principal interlocutor in Machiavelli's dialogue *Art
of War*, speaks these lines toward the beginning of this lively
dialogue, written in 1519 and 1520 and published in 1521. Tellingly, this was the only one of Machiavelli's major political works
that saw print publication in his lifetime, a fact that reinforces
a notion that has popped up elsewhere. Above all else, military
power—how one gains and deploys it—represents the most important element of Machiavelli's thought, a drumbeat without
which practically everything he wrote (outside the realm of the
comedies) loses its rhythm. And this quotation, with its exaltation of the "Romans," indicates one of Machiavelli's tics, something that grew more pronounced as he aged and was noticed
by contemporaries: the distant past was great, the present is
corrupt. Despite his views about the corruption of the present,
Machiavelli, determined as ever, sought to re-enter the world
of Florentine affairs any way he could. Machiavelli's *Art of War*

embodied one element of his manifold efforts, all set against the historical developments by which he was surrounded.

A lot had happened in Florence, Italy, and Europe in those fateful years after Machiavelli's arrest and imprisonment in 1513. The rehabilitation, rise, and continued ambitions of the Medici family took pride of place during this period. First, as we have seen, Giovanni de' Medici, one of Lorenzo the Magnificent's sons, ascended to the papal throne in 1513, an office he held until 1521. Thereafter was the short papacy of Adrian VI, followed by a second Medici pope, Cardinal Giulio de' Medici, the son of Lorenzo the Magnificent's assassinated brother Giuliano, who had fallen victim to the 1478 Pazzi conspiracy. Giulio took the papal name Clement VII and held office until his death in 1534. For two decades, then, the papacy, one of Europe's most uniquely important offices, lay in Medici hands, an advantage that they used to their benefit whenever and wherever they could. Leo, pleasure-loving as he was, was said (by a Venetian ambassador) to have uttered the immortal line: "Since God gave us the papacy, let us enjoy it."[2] Clement, more cautious in character, became a cardinal in 1513. During his cousin's pontificate, he held a number of important functions, including directing papal policy toward England and, importantly for our purposes, taking over some practical responsibilities in Florence when the occasion arose.

As to Florence, 1513 also saw another Medici, Lorenzo de' Medici (the grandson of Lorenzo the Magnificent), return to power as a "leading citizen," a development felicitous to some, odious to others. He too pursued the Medici drive toward expansion, desiring, and with the help of his uncle the pope, achieving the title of duke of Urbino in 1516. It was to him, in fact, that Machiavelli wound up dedicating *The Prince*, in the hope, vain in retrospect, that Lorenzo might become the sought-after redeemer of Italy for whom *The Prince*'s final lines cry out so urgently. As duke of Urbino he married a daughter of the count of Auvergne, with whom he had a daughter, Catherine de' Medici, who would later become queen of France. Lorenzo, however, was not the kind of forceful, spirited leader whose contours Machiavelli had outlined in *The Prince*. Twenty-one days after his daughter was born, Lorenzo died of syphilis, the result of his dedication to lust rather than state building. And in any case, he did that worst of things in the complex social economy of Florentine leadership: he absented himself for too long. For the truth was that despite the Medici return, the city hadn't settled on any definitive form of government. The Medici, acknowledged as Florence's leading citizens due to papal backing, had the advantage in Florence. Still, to exercise real power one needed to be present, to be part of the fray, and to engage in the give and take of Florentine public life. Lorenzo spent too much time away from Florence to retain the sort of political legitimacy that Florentine public life required. He came back a bit before he died, but by then he lived in practical seclusion from the rest of the city, styling himself a prince and thereby alienating many of Florence's leading citizens until his death in 1519.

◆ ◆ ◆

It was during these dramatic years, as we have seen, that Machiavelli frequented the Rucellai gardens. He also used this period (and his network of friends, many also frequenters of the

Rucellai gardens), to regain at least some of the status he had enjoyed before 1513. From this perspective, Lorenzo's death in 1519 represented a golden opportunity, all the more so since in that year Cardinal Giulio, the pope's cousin, came back to Florence to take things in hand and restore the Medici reputation there, which had suffered under Lorenzo, even among some traditional Medici allies. Giulio accomplished this task with aplomb, his quiet and studious nature suited to the mission.

Many of Florence's leading citizens, first off, simply wanted to be heard, and Giulio was prepared to grant them the audiences they desired. He was careful with public funds. He deliberately drew back from the "princely" conduct that Lorenzo had started to embrace, choosing to dress and live modestly, so that the symbolic aspects might emerge clearly: the Medici would lead in the way they had during the mythical golden days, acting like other leading citizens. He considered a number of proposals for governmental reforms that would enlarge the number of potentially politically active citizens and, by eliminating a restrictive dowry law that limited the size of citizen dowries, allowed up-and-coming newly wealthy citizens to make the kinds of matches for their children that they desired and could afford.[3] One contemporary historian commented that Giulio was "most humane in his deeds" and someone who "conversed willingly with smart and learned men in any profession."[4] One of the men with whom Giulio conversed was Machiavelli.

Machiavelli's friends had prepared the ground by writing letters and talking him up at the papal court in Rome. Finally Machiavelli's lukewarm relationship with the Medici seemed to be heating up, as Giulio granted Machiavelli an audience in May

of 1520. What precisely passed between the two men is unknown, but it can be well imagined that at least part of what
they discussed had to do with Machiavelli's work in progress.
The *Art of War* would see print publication about two years
later, but Machiavelli was working on it then, and it is a dialogue worth pausing a bit to understand. Set in the Rucellai
gardens, the *Art of War* is dedicated to Lorenzo Strozzi, the
friend in fact who had facilitated Machiavelli's meeting with
the Medici. The other interlocutors are Cosimo Rucellai and
a series of younger men, all of them real historical figures. Fabrizio and his interlocutors discuss practical details: how soldiers should be selected, armed, and trained; how battalions
ought to be arranged; how armies travel and what sort of provisions they should have; and so on. The quotation above—"I
won't ever depart from my Romans"—is uttered by the interlocutor Fabrizio Colonna, a well-known military captain and,
here, a stand-in for Machiavelli's views, especially during the
lengthy expository sections of the dialogue. Fabrizio, close to
the outset of the work, utters a lament that is pure Machiavelli:
he wonders why it is that today's leaders imitate the ancients
in art and culture but not when it comes to ordering their states,
the greater part of which effort must, as always, be devoted to
military affairs.

But that quotation can be paired with another, much later
in the work, when Fabrizio is discussing encampments: "Because in this narration of mine I want that the Romans be imitated, I shall not depart from their method of encampment,
even if I will not follow all of their rules, but will adopt instead
whatever parts of them that seem to me to be adaptable to
modern times."[5] In other words, Machiavelli is again concerned

that he not be pigeonholed as "the writer who slavishly imitates the Romans." He is looking for the practical matters that made the Romans great during the early Republic (for Machiavelli, this means before the Gracchi brothers, who were active in the late second century BC and whose radical land distribution policies engendered the first large-scale public violence in Rome for almost four centuries—after that, it was all downhill). Principally, the Romans' main advantage in this early period was that they had citizen armies composed *not* of men who made soldiering a profession but who would be just as inclined, after service in a battle, to want to go back home to their farms or trades. They were obliged to serve when called on but never formed a standing professional army, something that, once it did occur, inevitably gave the army far more power than it ought to have, and led to the almost constant assassination of emperors once the Praetorian guard came to great prominence in the first century AD. The Roman armies during this earlier, classic period had the use of ancient Roman religion: "With the greatest ceremony, they made their soldiers swear obedience to military discipline, so that, were they to contravene it, they would have to fear not only laws and men, but also God."[6]

What Machiavelli wanted was a political culture that would allow citizens from the city (for cavalry) and from the countryside (for infantry) to be recruited for military service, to be called up when necessary and drilled on days off from work. Machiavelli had invested much of his own time and mental energy in doing something just like this, as we have seen, with his most noteworthy success having been the Pisan campaign, though there had also been a failure, when his army was defeated in 1512 at Prato, outside of Florence, a defeat that led to the end of the Soderini regime and the re-entry of the Medici. So the issue was complicated. Yet he had an abiding faith that only if Florentine and Italian leaders encouraged the cultivation and growth of true citizen militias would Italy ever be able to resist the incursion of foreign powers. Instead of going this route, Machiavelli suggests that Italy's leadership class, having grown effete, has come to depend on professional mercenary captains, who have no loyalty to anything beyond being paid.

Now, if one notices similarities to *The Prince*, it is because the basic conceptions undergirding the *Art of War* are part of the same Machiavellian thought world—and in any case it should be remembered that Machiavelli did not actually print *The Prince* in his lifetime. His *Art of War* ends with the same sort of hope for redemption as does *The Prince*, for Fabrizio believes that real, ancient military discipline can be restored, since "this province"—Fabrizio means Italy—"seems born to resuscitate dead things, as one has seen in the cases of poetry, painting, and sculpture."[7] All it would take would be the right leaders, who could transfer all the energy behind the Renaissance of art and literature into a Renaissance of political—which meant military—culture. The *Art of War* became a classic, appreciated by the great theorist of modern warfare von Clausewitz (who famously said that war is politics continued by other means and called Machiavelli a "very sound judge of military matters"), eventually finding a place in the library of Thomas Jefferson.[8]

So the *Art of War* must have been one of the things on Machiavelli's mind when he spoke to Cardinal Giulio de' Medici.

Their conversation bore fruit for Machiavelli, as we can see from the commissions that emerged from it. Or rather, there was one main commission. With his friends' encouragement and to show his talents as a historian, Machiavelli had written a kind of audition piece. Called *The Life of Castruccio Castracani*, it had to do with the stormy life of an early fourteenth-century Italian *condottiere*, who became lord of Lucca and then Pisa, only to lose them after German backers withdrew their support. It was a dramatic tale and one that Machiavelli told with brio. *The Life of Castruccio* successfully impressed its intended audience, his friends and supporters who could lobby the Medici. So it was that Machiavelli, when all was said and done and after all the letters of recommendation and backstairs contacts, was hired by the head officials of the University of Florence, *ad componendum annalia et cronacas florentinas, et alia faciendum*—"to compose annals and chronicles of Florence, and to do other things"—as the Latin of his contract says.[9] Machiavelli was to be paid relatively little, about half of what he had earned when he held his official position as secretary. But it was enough. What it meant was that Machiavelli was asked, with Medici support, to become the official historian of Florence, a position that a number of former chancellors of Florence had held. Thus he could feel part of the system again, and the Medici, who were not yet ready to trust him with a powerful political position, could be seen as nourishing the talents of one of their city's finest writers. His *Florentine Histories*—again, unpublished during his lifetime—represent his final masterpiece.

Machiavelli's contract did say that he could be asked "to do other things" and asked he certainly was. The most notable of these involved Machiavelli sketching out a *Discourse on Florentine Affairs after the Death of Lorenzo* ("Lorenzo" being Lorenzo de' Medici, duke of Urbino, who died in 1519).[10] The idea, requested by Cardinal Giulio, was to present a draft governmental system for Florence that would account for the changes the city had undergone, the presence of the Medici, and provisions for future governance. This prospective constitutional opinion was something that Pope Leo X himself wanted to see, since he sought to find ways to ensure both power for his family and a workable governing system for Florence. Machiavelli suggested far-reaching changes, keeping only the *Gonfaloniere,* to be elected for at least two or three years, if not for life. And he would replace the usual magistracies with a large group of citizens whom Leo would select, who would serve for life. Thus Machiavelli presented a hybrid of the Venetian system (where a closed number of citizens served for a long period) and the Savonarolan re-organization of government (where power was given to a large council of citizens). All of this, to be sure, was to be supervised and watched over by the Medici. But there was one little hook: Machiavelli encouraged Leo to dissolve this system after his own and his cousin Giulio's natural death and thereafter to give Florence back "her liberty." In other words, Florence needed—for now—the stability that only a closed system combined with strong Medici leadership could provide. But thereafter, it should revert to its more traditional form with its traditional magistracies.

Machiavelli's proposal did not go anywhere, and it was in any case one of a number that the Medici solicited. If it had had a chance, that chance went south dramatically when in 1522 yet another anti-Medici conspiracy was uncovered, this time planned by some of the younger members of the Rucellai gardens. Once again, Machiavelli lost out by association, and though this time there was neither torture nor imprisonment, his chances at rising to a position of real political prominence came to an end for the foreseeable future. But he did still have his contract, and he began to work in earnest on the *Florentine Histories*, a project that would take him three years.

The *Florentine Histories* can be set alongside *The Prince* and the *Discourses* as an exemplary, lasting work. Dedicated to Pope Clement VII (who when a cardinal had been instrumental in getting Machiavelli this commission), Machiavelli's *Florentine Histories* take readers through Florence and its history from the fall of the Roman Empire until 1492 and the death of Lorenzo the Magnificent. The *Histories*, like his other two great works, awaited print publication until after Machiavelli's death, seeing the light only in 1532. By the 1520s, when Machiavelli wrote the *Histories*, his thoughts on politics and history had matured, and in some respects the *Histories* can seem almost like a case study.

Machiavelli's preface tells us a great deal about his motivations in writing this work. Others who had occupied chancery posts in Florence had written of Florentine history. The two most notable were Leonardo Bruni and Poggio Bracciolini, each of whom served as chancellor in the fifteenth century (Bruni from 1410 to 1411 and 1427 to 1444, the year of his death, Poggio from 1453 until his death in 1459). Each had written histories of Florence in elegant humanist Latin. Machiavelli says in his own preface that his original intention had been to write the history of Florence only from the year 1434 on, the year, that is, in which Cosimo de' Medici came to prominence as Florence's leading citizen. His assumption had been that Bruni and Poggio would have covered the earlier years thoroughly. But, Machiavelli writes, "having read carefully their writings to see precisely what techniques of style and organization they employed when writing—so that in imitating them our own work might find better favor among readers—I found that they were quite diligent when it came to describing the wars that the Florentines waged with princes and foreign enemies. But when it came to civil discord and enmities internal to the city of Florence and the consequent effects of these things, they were basically silent about the latter and said little to nothing about the former, in such a way that to readers it offered neither utility nor pleasure."[11] Machiavelli had done his homework, in other words, having scrutinized the work of Florence's two great and respected historians. But his point is that they missed one thing, principally: conflict, an element that we have seen is central to Machiavelli's view of how cities function, especially republics like Florence.

Florence, he suggests, has had many internal divisions, first among the nobles, then among the nobles and the "people"—the *popolo*—and then finally among the *popolo* and the common people.[12] One simply could not write conflict out of Florentine history, since conflict propelled change, and change is the stuff of which history is made. Florence's seemingly never-ending constitutional reforms, its reasons for waging war at any given moment, and its relations with external powers: all these and more needed to be told with conflict as the central vantage point. Machiavelli's insights regarding the perennial presence of conflict in human affairs emerged both in *The Prince*, where he spoke of the different "humors" in any given city (whereby the powerful want to oppress and the people want not to be oppressed) and in the *Discourses*, where his careful reading of Livy revealed the constant jockeying among classes in the ancient

Roman republic. Here, in his *Histories*, he feels obligated to use those insights and apply them practically. He has written eight books, he says. The first four cover all the unforeseen events in Italy after the fall of the Roman Empire, moving to Florence until 1434. The last four books deal with Florence in context from 1434 to 1492, the death of Lorenzo.

Machiavelli has a theory of history: it is cyclical. He explains it best at the beginning of book 5, where he writes that "for the most part, provinces"—he means here "states," or "countries"—"in the changes that they undergo, move from order to disorder, only to pass yet again from disorder to order."[13] States rise and they fall, in other words, taking their beginnings from the efforts of heroic men who possess *virtù*—and here Machiavelli means old school, masculine, martial virtue, with emphasis on the *vir*—"man": "Virtue gives birth to tranquility, tranquility to leisure, leisure to disorder, disorder to ruin; and similarly from ruin, order is born, from order virtue, from virtue, glory and good fortune."[14] Another way to say this? "Prudent men have observed that literature comes after arms, and that in provinces and cities military captains arise before philosophers."[15] The sentiment is wholly characteristic of Machiavelli's thought: military power is most important and can guarantee security, but once this security is achieved, people tend to forget their military obligations, outsource their wars, and, basically, grow soft.

There was an important ancient historian, Polybius (who lived in the second century BC), who had himself propounded a cyclical theory of history in his *Histories* (six books of which survive). Polybius had written about Roman history in Greek, a language that Machiavelli did not know. But Polybius's

Histories had been translated into Latin bit by bit in the fifteenth century. And the incomplete but important book 6 (where the theory of cyclical change finds greatest expression) was turned into Latin by the fifteenth century's greatest classical scholar, Angelo Poliziano, whose memorable account of the Pazzi conspiracy was only one of a number of works he produced in his lifetime. So Machiavelli could have read Polybius. Yet, as in the case of other classical sources, it is beside the point when examining Machiavelli to rely too heavily on a "find the source" mentality in explaining his thinking and procedure. Powers rise and fall. It is not that complicated. What is more interesting, in Machiavelli's view, is seeing the particular ways powers rise and fall, how historical particularities can inflect the general, seemingly inevitable trajectory of cyclical growth and decline. To understand what Machiavelli thinks about Florence in this regard, three aspects of his *Histories* come to the fore: the presence of the papacy in Italy, Machiavelli's comparison of ancient Rome to Florence, and, finally, the presence of the Medici as leading citizens in the fifteenth century.

Just as Machiavelli highlighted the exceptional nature of the papacy in *The Prince*, devoting a whole chapter to "Ecclesiastical Princedoms," so too in the *Histories* does he single out the papacy as an institution that has had noticeable effects in Italy. For Machiavelli the roots went deep, far back into history, to the time when ancient Rome suffered incursions by "barbarians," meaning invaders who came from beyond the Italian peninsula. This period would be roughly around the time of the Emperor Honorius, who ruled from 395 to 423. Momentous changes (*variazioni*) occurred, Machiavelli suggests, not only in forms of government and leadership, but also in "laws, customs, way of life, religion, language, dress, names."[16] Some cities declined in this era, others grew (Florence was among the latter), and there were new names introduced, not just for cities, but even for "lakes, rivers, seas, and men."[17]

"Yet among all these changes, the change in religion was no less important."[18] Christianity, by way of contrast with the customs of the ancient Roman religion, offered miracles and in that fashion attracted attention. But Christianity was divided for many years into different sects, divisions that caused incalculable suffering. By the sixth century, ever more change occurred, especially in the way popes were regarded. In their earliest years, the successors to St. Peter gained their status through living a holy life and performing miracles. But Constantine moved the center of the Empire to Byzantium in the early fourth century, and then the Ostrogothic ruler Theodoric, king of Italy from 493 to 526, moved his power center from Rome to Ravenna. These developments led to the popes in Rome having more temporal power, enlarging their dominion, but never becoming powerful enough to sustain their rule without outside help.

So: "From this point on, all the wars that the barbarians waged in Italy were for the most part caused by the popes, and all the barbarians that inundated Italy were, again for the most part, called in by the popes. This way of proceeding continues even now, something that has kept and continues to keep Italy disunited and weak."[19] Throughout Machiavelli's work there is this sense that Christianity as practiced has not served Italy well. In *The Prince*, he suggested that the institution of the papacy was a particular kind of princedom, whose princes, the popes, "have states and do not defend them, have subjects and do not govern them," and yet still wield immense worldly power.[20] In the *Discourses*, he suggested that Christianity's value system was off: by glorifying humility and de-emphasizing worldly fame, it did not inspire great, daring, and aggressive feats among political actors. And here, in the *Histories*, Machiavelli documents many examples of popes causing mischief. In the thirteenth century, for example—to fast-forward a bit— Rome was coming under the political sway of the French king Charles of Anjou, who held the title to Naples and Sicily and had recently become a Roman senator. Machiavelli describes the very short-lived Pope Adrian V (Pope only from July 11 to August 18, 1276), in this way, highlighting Adrian's relations with Charles of Anjou: "And since Charles was in Rome, governing it through the office of senator that he held, the pope could not tolerate Charles's power. He left and went to live in Viterbo, and solicited the [German] Emperor Rudolf to come down into Italy against Charles. It is in this fashion that the popes, now for the sake of religion, now for their own ambition, did not cease to call new men into Italy and to encourage new wars. And as soon as they made one prince powerful they regretted it and sought his ruin, nor could they allow others to have power over that province that they themselves could not hold, owing to their own weakness."[21] Classic Machiavelli. The *Histories* are replete with these sorts of examples of popes behaving badly, in Machiavelli's opinion.

If part of Italy's weakness and disunity has had to do with the presence of the papacy, Florence has some particularities of its own that Machiavelli believes are worth noting— particularities that come into relief when compared to ancient Rome. The comparison occurs in the first chapter of book 3, where Machiavelli begins with one of his core beliefs: "The serious and natural enmities that exist between the people and the nobles, which are occasioned by the nobility's desire to command and the people's desire not to obey, represent the reason for all the evils that arise in cities, since this diversity of humors nourishes everything else that causes disturbances in republics."[22] He starts, in other words, with a general principle we have seen elsewhere. In cities, there will always be different classes of people, and they will be forever in competition with each other. Conflict is unavoidable. How conflict is resolved represents the key problem that states (and those that govern them) need to address, and this is where the comparison of ancient Rome to Florence comes into relief. Both cities suffered disunity because of class conflict, but the conflict had different effects, since "in Rome the enmities that arose between the people and the nobles were resolved by argument, whereas in Florence they were resolved by fighting; those in Rome ended up in the promulgation of law, those in Florence in the exile and the death of many citizens; those in Rome helped martial virtue grow, whereas those in Florence led to its complete extinction."[23] There was something about the ancient Romans that led them to take the right path when dealing as a society with class conflict, or with—in Machiavelli's terms—the "enmities" between classes.

The comparison then goes in a surprising direction, at least for modern readers. For these enmities also led, in the end, to the Romans moving from "an equality among the citizenry to a very great inequality," whereas the class enmities led the Florentines "from an inequality to a marvelous equality." Machiavelli says that these different effects came from what must have been the different desires and goals that the Romans and the Florentines possessed. The "people" in Rome "wanted to enjoy the highest honors together with the nobles," whereas the "people" in Florence "fought to govern by themselves, without any participation from the nobles."[24] Since the Romans' desire was much more reasonable, it was acceptable to the nobles to share power. "On the other hand, the desire of the Florentine people was injurious and unjust, so that the nobles readied their defenses with ever more force, from which came bloodshed and exiles of the citizenry. And those laws that were then created, were devised not for the common good but only in favor of the victors."[25] Needless to say, there is a lot of history compressed into this short passage.

As to the Romans, Machiavelli was referring to developments that took centuries. Modern scholars of Roman antiquity term these developments the "conflict of the orders," a long process at the end of which those of nonaristocratic status got a seat at the table, were allowed to serve as consuls, and were allowed to take part in government. As to Florence, Machiavelli is alluding to the *Ordinances of Justice*, a set of Florentine laws passed in the last decade of the thirteenth century. The effort was to disallow participation in governance by aristocratic families and ensure that only those who belonged to Florence's system of craft guilds could participate. The theory was that the aristocratic families were too warlike, always carrying out vendettas, whereas the rising merchant class was deemed more harmonious. The "people" belonged to the various Florentine guilds, which included professional specialties and trades, from notaries, bankers, and pharmacists, on the high end, to butchers, blacksmiths, and shoemakers, on the lower end.

Both of these developments, the Roman and the Florentine, were endlessly complex and never possessed the static nature that Machiavelli's short description implied. And in any case

Machiavelli's point is that it is natural that there will be different classes and equally natural that they will come into conflict. You cannot wish these divisions away, as the Florentines tried to do to their detriment, with their *Ordinances* and with other measures designed to suppress the power of the *grandi*. Rather, through the right sorts of laws (which would themselves arise from the right sort of public culture), you can manage these conflicts. But it was precisely this turning away from a culture of law buttressed by strong, internal military power that represented Florence's biggest failing and left it vulnerable to outside attack. Though Machiavelli is careful about how he chooses his words, it is clear enough that, closer to his own day, it was the Medici family whose politics put the final nail in the coffin in the fifteenth century, concluding the momentous epoch that came to an end in 1494 and whose hallmark was the arrival of the French.

Serious analysis of the Medici begins in book 7 of the *Histories*, the penultimate book. As ever, Machiavelli enunciates a general statement, and, again, it will seem familiar: "First I want to point out that those who hope that a republic can be unified are greatly fooled in that hope. It is true that certain divisions harm republics and others help them. Those divisions that harm republics are those that are accompanied by factions and partisans, whereas those that help a republic are those that are maintained without factions and partisans."[26] Here, then, as Machiavelli is approaching the Medici, he starts to clarify what sorts of societal divisions, inevitable as these are, can be sustained in a functioning society.

What he means by "factions" (he uses the word *sette*, "sects," literally) and "partisans" can be located in the realm of personal

politics. This is to say that "sects" form around individual interests and personal loyalties, rather than around the medium-
and long-term interests of the state. From this state of affairs
arise "partisans," immoderate political actors who by definition
put personal loyalties beyond anything else. Machiavelli goes
on to say that no founder of a republic can eliminate conflicts.
But he can see to it that factions are avoided. In other words
(and yet again), there are things within a leader's power that
can be done to avoid negative political consequences. In this
case the notional citizen is not a prince but the citizen of a republic desiring to have a positive impact on his city and its political life.

There are "public" and "private" ways to have success:

> Publicly, citizens acquire a reputation by winning a
> battle, taking possession of a town, carrying out a dip-
> lomatic mission with expedition and prudence, and ad-
> vising the republic wisely and successfully. Privately,
> citizens acquire a reputation by helping this or that
> citizen, defending him from magistrates, lending him
> money, procuring him offices he does not deserve, and
> with games and gifts gratifying the masses. It is from
> this way of behaving that there arise factions and par-
> tisans. As much as a reputation earned in this latter
> fashion is offensive, so too is the other way beneficial,
> since it is founded on a common, rather than a private,
> good.[27]

The basic distinction emerges as "public" versus "private" when
it comes to that all-important commodity in political life: rep-

utation. For reputations inspire trust, fear, love, respect, and hatred, depending on how they are acquired, and those citizens who wish to play a leading role in a republic must manage their own reputations accordingly.

As to the "public" manner of gaining a good reputation, it is impossible to imagine that Machiavelli did not have himself in mind, if we take a close look at his language, combine this analysis with the facts of his own life, and try, fancifully to be sure, to think in his own, internal voice:

"Publicly, citizens gain a reputation by winning a battle." Check. See my victory at Pisa in 1509.

"Taking possession of a town." Check. See Pisa, again.

"Carrying out a diplomatic mission with expedition and prudence." Check. See my over forty missions outside of Florence on behalf of my city.

"And advising the republic wisely and successfully." Check. See my reorganization of the Florentine military, my countless, well-written, and witty reports that I sent back from my missions to the leaders of my city, my efforts to rewrite Florence's laws in a prudential way, taking into account both current conditions and the sage counsel of the ancients, and my never-ending efforts to help my city, whose leading citizens just won't listen to me, but I will keep trying anyway.

That is going too far, of course. Still, fanciful reconstruction of Machiavelli's private and ultimately unknowable psychology aside, it is clear enough that he saw powerful linkages between the way he lived his public life before his 1513 catastrophes and the ideal comportment of a patriotic citizen. Agree or disagree with the techniques, theoretical underpinnings, and final results in any or all cases, the truth is that he did serve his city by concentrating on military affairs, strategic diplomacy, and constitutional reform (keeping in mind, in the latter category, that many others were in the mix as well). He did, in short, live the life of a "public"-minded person.

On the other side, there is the "private" manner of gaining prominence in a republic. The tone of Machiavelli's description is negative:

"Helping *this or that* citizen" (as if the choice of whom to help is indiscriminate and instrumental, undertaken out of a desire to tie the citizen in question into a patronage relationship rather than for the good of the republic).

"Lending him money." Despite Florence's strong identification as a city of bankers, the specter of the sin of usury, lending money for interest, always hovered over these interactions, so that mentioning money lending had less-than-positive associations. And it goes without saying that there were no greater bankers, no greater moneylenders, than the Medici.

"Procuring him offices he does not deserve." Public offices should serve the public good, and therefore those who are chosen for these offices should be the best available, not (necessarily) friends or anyone else chosen for anything other than a meritocratic reason.

"And with games and gifts gratifying the masses." This classic complaint, that leaders sometimes dazzle the people with spectacles, is at least as old as the first-century AD Latin poet Juvenal, who satirized the "bread and circuses" with which the Roman emperors kept the people satisfied, compliant, and docile.[28] But didn't Machiavelli himself say that the people enjoy spectacles? That was in *The Prince*, of course, and here we are on the presumably purer terrain of republics. Yet there must have been a part of Machiavelli that knew that his idealized opposition between "public" and "private" seemed more ideal than real, that you could not just imagine away the patronage-based social system, the massive banking operations—along with strategic private moneylending—that were at the beating heart of the Florentine economy, and the strategic use of public offices to create political alliances. That was the world in which he lived. He must have known all this. He did know all this.

Machiavelli is setting up this opposition for a reason. History in Machiavelli's day was considered a genre of rhetoric, meant to tell a story and in so doing to persuade readers of positions, theories, and conclusions that an author wanted to communicate. And here, what Machiavelli wants to communicate is that the heyday of Medici rule in Florence did not serve the republic well, weakening its institutions and capacities—from 1434, when Cosimo de' Medici came back from exile and built his lasting political coalition, to 1494 and the disastrous arrival of the French, and then the Spanish, and then everybody else.

The framing device is the key here. To an attentive reader, it is obvious which of the two ways of being a citizen, public or private, is better: public, at least in an ideal republic. So it is striking when, in the immediately succeeding chapter, Machiavelli describes Florence in the 1440s and early 1450s as having had two leading citizens, Cosimo de' Medici and Neri Capponi. (The Capponi were another leading Florentine family, less wealthy than the Medici but with long roots in Florence.) We learn that, "of the two, Neri was one of those who had acquired his reputation in a public fashion, in such a way that he had many friends and few partisans. Cosimo on the other hand, having within his power both the public and private methods, had both friends and partisans."[29] Coming right after Machiavelli's praise of purely public citizenship, this description is hardly flattering to Cosimo. And indeed, in narrating events after Capponi's death in 1455, Machiavelli suggests that what had been a tenuous balance fell into disequilibrium, as Cosimo's powerful friends, now no longer afraid of opposition from the Capponi party, sought to aggrandize themselves and reduce Cosimo's power, so that Florence was hurt by the power of factionalism. Their actions led Cosimo to recur to the Renaissance equivalent of stuffing the ballot box. The Florentine system of picking members for governmental positions functioned notionally by lot, with the names of eligible participants—supposedly selected by neutral observers—picked out of bags. And Cosimo "well knew that he ran no risk governing in this fashion, since the voting bags were full of his friends' names."[30] Then as the Cosimo years wore on, tax breaks were given to friends, honest government was corrupted, and different, more grandiose styles of public consumption emerged.

All of this stood in stark contrast to the way Cosimo behaved. Indeed, reading Machiavelli's biographical description of Cosimo, one finds that positive qualities abound. Cosimo is described as follows: "For someone outside of the military profession, Cosimo was the most renowned and famous citizen, not only in Florence but in the memory of any other city. For not only did he surpass everyone else in his own day when it came to authority and wealth, he also did so when it came to generosity and prudence."[31] Fair enough. But Machiavelli does say that "among all the other qualities that rendered him the 'prince' in his native land, the most important thing was

that he surpassed all others in being generous and magnificent."[32] These are positive qualities, to be sure. Yet, an attentive
reader's ears would perk up, were he to read what comes next.

After Cosimo's death, when his accounts were being settled,
it was discovered that "there was no citizen of any reputation
who had not been loaned exceedingly large sums of money by
Cosimo."[33] Not only that, but "many times without even being
asked, he would help out a nobleman when he sensed the
need."[34] Read one way, this is a simple description of a generous
man, helping people when they needed it and aware enough to
help people without their even needing to ask. Read in the context of Machiavelli's earlier description of the public versus
the private citizen, this generosity could be seen as having a
less-than-positive civic side, as gaining partisans for Cosimo,
rather than cultivating disinterested citizens for Florence.
And then of course there is Machiavelli's use of the word
"prince"—*principe*—in Italian. It is rendered here in quotation marks simply to show that Machiavelli did not mean a
hereditary prince, for the word could indeed mean "first," as in
"first citizen." Still, in the context of all of Machiavelli's other
work and given political Florence's historic dislike of the idea
of one-man rule, one intuits that Machiavelli is sending messages. At the very least, recalling the dialogical sensibility that
pervaded so much Renaissance thought, he could be read as
doing so.

When it comes to Cosimo's magnificence, there too, there
are two sides to the same coin. On the one hand, Cosimo restored or rebuilt numerous churches in Florence and its territories, commissioned altars, and offered generous patronage,
thereby beautifying the city. On the other, he built a number

of private homes, including some outside of the city. These were "palaces appropriate for kings, rather than for private citizens . . . and even though these houses, along with his other work and activities, were kingly, and even though he alone, really, was 'prince' in Florence, nevertheless everything was tempered by his prudence to such an extent that he never seemed to go beyond that special modesty appropriate for a citizen. . . . For he knew that doing things that are out of the ordinary, things that are constantly observed, excites more envy among men than things that seem to be done with integrity and modesty."[35] Here Machiavelli's account is delicate. On the one hand, he offers sincere praise and admiration for the way Cosimo's patronage transformed the city's cultural landscape. On the other, there are those telling little clues ("palaces appropriate for kings") that, combined with what Machiavelli tells us elsewhere, are enough to communicate that, in his view, Cosimo's legacy was not ideal.

Regarding Cosimo, Machiavelli says that, "with respect to states ruled by princes or in the case of republics, no one equaled him in his day for intelligence. . . . In the midst of such a variety of fortune and such an unstable citizenry, he held on to a state for thirty-one years since, because he was so very prudent, he recognized evils at a distance."[36] The result was that despite Florence's tumultuous political life, Cosimo held power for quite a long time. "The reason was that he was tremendously prudent and recognized problems from a distance, so that he afforded himself the time either to keep them from growing or to prepare himself in such a way that, even if those problems did grow, he would remain safe."[37] This type of political prudence is dear to Machiavelli, who elsewhere says that this quality is one of the things that made the ancient Romans great during their period of highest political ascendency. But Machiavelli also suggests, in his *Discourses*, that governments that depend for their vitality on one person's charisma are inherently weak and that a truly healthy governmental system is one that is shaped by its leader (whether a prince or a leading citizen in a republic) in such a way that when he dies the state can be maintained.[38] A careful reader could infer that Cosimo, despite his formidable financial resources, prudence, and general political skills, did not fit Florence out well for the future.

The same could be said about Lorenzo the Magnificent, Cosimo's grandson and the other great fifteenth-century Medici leader, around whose memory, in Machiavelli's own day, in the early sixteenth century, a cult of greatness was in flower, as the myth of the golden age of Lorenzo grew. Writing about Lorenzo, Machiavelli recognizes something with which modern historians tend to agree: that with the rise of Lorenzo the Magnificent, the Medici family began to look outside of Florence to make its name greater and to increase its influence throughout Europe. Lorenzo "turned his heart to the enterprise of making himself and his city great. He married off his first-born son to Alfonsina, the daughter of the knight Orsini."[39] Step one: create a marriage alliance of your own, Florentine family, to a member of the Roman nobility (in this case the Orsini, an old Roman family). Cosimo had never done this with his children, seeking instead marriages within the Florentine clans—good marriages, to be sure, but still intra-Florentine. Step two: "then he had his second son, Giovanni, elevated to the cardinalate."[40] Giovanni, of course, would later become Pope Leo X. Engineering Giovanni's rise to the rank of cardinal at such a young age was "all the more noteworthy," Machiavelli remarks drily, "insofar as it was unprecedented, since he was raised to such a rank even though he was not yet fourteen years old. This was indeed the ladder that would allow his family to scale the heavens, as indeed occurred."[41]

Lorenzo was not the best custodian of his own finances. "As to his private affairs he was most unfortunate when it came to financial matters, owing to the disorderly way his administrators behaved, who conducted themselves rather like princes than private citizens."[42] Think of *The Prince*, where Machiavelli devotes quite a bit of space to the importance of picking good advisors. Imagine what he must have really thought of Lorenzo. And Lorenzo's poor management of his finances and unskilled choice of allies affected more than just the Medici family: "as a result, his native city was compelled to support him with quite a bit of money."[43] Private mismanagement harmed public finances. What could be a worse critique? All the more so, since Machiavelli's opinion seems to be that on important matters Lorenzo allowed his advisors to run away with things he should have taken care of himself.

Needless to say, Machiavelli makes sure to point out the positive accomplishments with which Lorenzo might be credited: he refounded the University of Florence, strengthening its main branch in Pisa and bringing to Florence leading humanist intellectuals. He patronized the arts, supported writers, and wrote notable poetry himself. Yet again, if one couples these positive attributes with what Machiavelli writes elsewhere, Lorenzo seems less positive, for the leaders of states Machiavelli really admires were hardnosed military types. One recalls what he writes elsewhere in the *Florentine Histories* to the effect that philosophers only come later in a city's evolution. By this standard, Lorenzo seems, if not weak and effete, somewhat of a dabbler and a dandy, unserious and not up to the tasks the times presented him. And in any case, what was his legacy? Again, a city held together by personal charisma rather than lasting institutions, a city whose institutions were thrown into severe disarray as soon as it was met with a serious challenge in 1494, two years after Lorenzo's death.

There would be a lot more to remark upon, and there certainly is much more to appreciate in the *Florentine Histories*: dramatic narratives of battles, clear-eyed accounts of how Florence's governmental system evolved, and insightful character sketches toward the end of fulfilling Machiavelli's promise, at the outset, that he would illuminate Florence's internecine power struggles (something he does brilliantly by capturing the psychological essences of the political actors under examination). Though the *Histories* went unprinted in his lifetime, Machiavelli was permitted to present a manuscript dedication copy to Pope Clement VII in 1525, that very same Giulio de' Medici who, when a cardinal, had facilitated Machiavelli's partial rehabilitation.

If Pope Clement had a detailed reaction, it has gone unrecorded, but he did thereafter provide Machiavelli with an increase in pay and moreover sent him to the Romagna, to work with his friend Guicciardini, then the governor of that region on behalf of the Papal States. Machiavelli's charge was to help plan a militia for the papacy as he had done for Florence over fifteen years earlier. But the early enthusiasm for the plan fizzled out. The Florentine state thenceforth employed him on some missions, including one to Venice, and Machiavelli was beginning to regain a public, political persona in Florence, such as he had dreamed of incessantly after his catastrophes. He was even elected to a governmental body designed to deal with fortifications.

Again, however, fickle fortune dealt Machiavelli another blow. Pope Clement had been an excellent cardinal, incisive in his dealings and intelligent in the causes he supported. As a pope, however, his indecisiveness cost him—and the city of Rome—dearly. In the constant, ever-shifting maneuvers among the various powers vying for control of Italy, Clement did not choose sides firmly or well. The long and the short of it was that the powerful Hapsburg ruler, Emperor Charles V, had his eye on dominion and empire. Finding Clement allied in a league against him, Charles's imperial troops approached, took, and sacked Rome on May 6, 1527. By this time the imperial army included a number of German hired soldiers, themselves followers of Martin Luther and his new version of Christianity—and thus no fans of what they saw as popish, decadent Rome. The sack was violent, costly, and humiliating to the Medici pope, who was forced to flee St. Peter's and hole up in the Castel Sant'Angelo, the ancient pagan mausoleum of the emperor Hadrian that, during the long Christian centuries, had been re-purposed as a papal fortress. Florence, of course, was dragged along in the bitter wake of this inundation, and the Medici regime there, in whose good graces Machiavelli had finally managed to insert himself, fell. Once again, he was out of a job. Though his friends in Florence lobbied to have him elected to the chancery again, his recent service to the ousted regime made him too hot to touch. Surely Machiavelli, who had thought so long and hard about fortune's wheel, must have laughed, if bitterly, in the midst of his disappointment. He did not have long to ponder these events: he was taken ill soon thereafter and on June 21, 1527, passed away due to a violent stomach ailment, possibly peritonitis.

8

Ghosts

. . .

There is a delightful Italian expression: *anche se non è vero, è ben trovato*, which means, more or less, "even if it's not true, it makes for a good story." One such story is a traditional one, mentioned in connection with Machiavelli's death since the early seventeenth century. Soon before he died, Machiavelli is said to have told friends of a dream he had, in which a vision presented itself. There were two groups of men, one of which consisted of figures poorly dressed and wretched, the other of men who, through their comportment and dress, appeared dignified and serious. Upon asking the first group who they were, Machiavelli received the response that they were the blessed, on their way to heaven. The second group, by contrast, comprised serious ancient thinkers such as Plato, Seneca, Plutarch, and Tacitus, who shared the merit of having written fundamental works on politics and history. They, however, identified themselves as the damned, on the way to Hades. Machiavelli told his friends that he preferred to go to hell, so that he might discuss politics with the ancient luminaries rather than be bored for eternity with the blessed.

No surprise, of course, that this tale circulated about Machiavelli, who was known to be openly contemptuous of the

Christianity of his day. Now there are no solid sources for this story close to Machiavelli's era (it first appeared in 1629), and indeed it is possible that Machiavelli did, on his deathbed, make a final confession to a priest.[1] That said, "Machiavelli's dream" makes for a good story. Perceptions, even those that are no more than traditional, are always meaningful, and in any case the dream allows us access to both the ghosts with which Machiavelli was surrounded in his own day and those that haunt his image even now.

As it did for so many Renaissance thinkers, antiquity haunted Machiavelli in ways too numerous to count. The powerful notion that "everything was better in the past" was not particular to the Renaissance, needless to say. It existed even in some of Machiavelli's favorite ancient sources, such as Livy himself, who began his historical account of ancient Rome by lamenting the rise in a taste for luxury that was infecting his contemporaries, in contrast to Rome's noble past, where "poverty went hand in hand with contentment."[2] Moreover, nostalgia is a natural human tendency, as we often look with rose-colored glasses at the past, choosing to remember the good, even as we selectively erase the bad.

But Machiavelli came to maturity at the tail end of the greatest period of literary and historical rediscovery the west had known. He did so in the city, Florence, which—for all that other Italian cities contributed to the Renaissance effort to recover and document the ancient Greco-Roman past—was Italy's most admired and envied cultural center. There can be no doubt that for Italian humanists—those thinkers in fifteenth-century Italy who devoted themselves to this recovery—these efforts allowed them, and human culture, to progress. Their discoveries on the page led to a mindset conducive to greater receptivity to other, later discoveries, whether these were the voyages to the "new" world (a "discovery," needless to say, only to Europeans and not to the native peoples they often violently displaced) or those of emerging natural science. Beyond discoveries, Renaissance humanism and its passion for the past led to new ways of thinking about history, with a better, more solid sense of historical context and new ways of conceptualizing human experience.

Machiavelli's relationship to Renaissance culture was ambivalent. On the one hand—and this is probably the most important thing to say about him—he was not a scholar. He was instead a professional man of action, quite learned and stunningly intelligent, but someone more comfortable, content, and enthusiastic when he was engaging in political life rather than writing about it. On the other, he was heir and beneficiary of the Latinate, classicizing learning that his era and city had bequeathed him. He was educated by a humanist teacher, showed early and abiding interest in classical literature, and came to see antiquity as one of the two most important elements by which he made sense of the world. The other, of course, was his contemporary experience in the messily unstable realm of politics and war. When Machiavelli told his friend Francesco Vettori that, in the evenings, he changed his clothes as he entered the "ancient courts of ancient men," there must have been more than a little rhetorical affectation there. (Did he do that every day? Did he really put on dress clothes?). But there is, as in all such affectations, a core of truth, in the sense that he clearly possessed a reverence for the ancient Roman past, a reverence that must have made the present seem paltry, weak, and the antithesis of imperial.

Then there was the ghost of the ideal world. If only the right leader, or the right governmental system, or both in some combination or another, could be found to cure the ills with which Florence was afflicted—ills that resonated outward to "Italy," which at the time represented a geographic, to an extent cultural, but not yet political unity. If only. One way to look at this notion of the ideal and the reverence in which it was held is to look back to a thinker Machiavelli probably knew, or at least knew of, when he was young: Angelo Poliziano. Poliziano, we recall, died in 1494 and had authored the dramatic account of the Pazzi conspiracy, that ill-fated plot that resulted in the assassination of Giuliano de' Medici, a plot from which his brother Lorenzo the Magnificent, also a target, escaped alive. Among Poliziano's many scholarly projects (in a career remarkably productive for someone who lived only forty years) was an early, 1479 translation from Greek into Latin of the *Handbook* of the ancient thinker Epictetus, active at the end of the first and early part of the second centuries AD.

Epictetus, a Stoic, was one of antiquity's firmest and most lasting advocates of the notion that you should worry only about what you can control, things like your opinions, impulses, and emotions. Self-cultivation was the key, and the ideal in this respect was what Epictetus and other Stoics termed a "sage," which is to say a person who had mastered this set of techniques perfectly, who never criticized anyone else, never felt grief, and was in complete control of his emotions. The "sage," however, was an ideal figure, someone who could not really be found in this world. What was important was the *notion* of the sage, the very idea that a person like this could be imagined as a perfect ideal toward which those interested in cultivating the good life could fruitfully aim. Machiavelli's thought, as we have seen, is inflected everywhere by Stoic commonplaces—in *The Prince*, for example, when he emphasizes that a prince should choose being feared over loved if a choice needed to be made, since he could control being feared but not being loved. But Machiavelli is unreflective concerning that other part of Stoicism, concerned with self-examination. His realism is a realism of politics, not of the human person. He is still able to conceive of the possibility of ideal solutions (an ideal prince, an ideal republic) to the problems of a world in which everything he had observed should have convinced him that these solutions were unlikely at best in his day, that "Italy" as such had no realistic hopes of competing against the other, larger, more centralized powers that were beginning to dominate European politics.

It is plausible that Machiavelli knew of Epictetus's *Handbook*, if not directly then indirectly, through the common premodern oral tradition. Again, however, he would not have needed it to understand its central messages, especially that closest to his own heart: concerning oneself with what one can control. This conception was a commonplace, and it was experience, rather than texts, that fixed it so firmly in Machiavelli's mind.

That other notion, the ideal, is much more complicated, and it is connected to the other ghost hovering over all of Machiavelli's work: Christianity. Again, his stance and situation are complicated. Outwardly it is easy. Both in his own texts and in what others say about him, there is no question that Machiavelli had no patience with the contemporary Christianity with which he was surrounded, that he was known to be, as his friend Guicciardini put it, of a *contraria professione*—a "contrary profession"—when it came to religion. He was part of a group of elite Italians, many of whom had spent time either in or around the papal court, who simply had no patience anymore with the papacy's, and hence Christianity's, worldly ambitions. That very same Francesco Guicciardini put his own feelings this way, in one of his *Ricordi*, or *Maxims*, that he composed throughout his life: "I don't know anyone who dislikes the ambition, the avarice, and the sensuality of priests more than I do. . . . Nevertheless, the position I have enjoyed with several popes has forced me to love their greatness for my own self-interest. If it weren't for this consideration, I would have loved Martin Luther as much as I love myself—not to be released from the laws taught by the Christian religion as it is normally interpreted and understood, but to see this band of ruffians reduced within their correct bounds."[3] Now Guicciardini did not make his *Ricordi* public in his lifetime. He clearly was speaking here in a private moment to his own private self, and in any case many of us have allowed ourselves confidential thoughts, sometimes shared with intimates. But without making too much of his statement here, we should also not make too little of it either.

The ghost of Christianity. Textbook accounts, at least until recently, used to speak of the Protestant Reformation shattering an ideal medieval Catholic unity, after Martin Luther in 1517 posted his "95 theses" objecting to certain Catholic teachings and practices on the door of Wittenberg Cathedral. But take a roughly two-hundred-year look backward from Machiavelli and Guicciardini's day. For most of the fourteenth century, from

1309 to 1378, to be exact, the papal court vacated Rome, the city where the first bishop of Rome, Saint Peter, was martyred. It was from Peter that all popes were thought to descend in apostolic succession, and Rome had become throughout the Middle Ages not only the papacy's traditional seat, but also the symbolic center of western Christendom. Then from 1378 to 1417 there were two, and for a few years three rival claimants to the papacy, with one observance in Rome, another in Avignon, and yet another in Pisa. And once the Roman Otto Colonna was elected pope as Martin V in 1417, the papacy was not really at home in Rome until 1443, owing to internecine fighting among Rome's leading families. Once it did establish itself again in Rome, it grew ever more secular with a marked increase in sale of offices and other forms of venality, so much so that there were significant, repeated, and forceful calls from within the Catholic Church itself for reform. "Unity" is not the word one would use to describe Christianity before the Reformation. So the church itself formed part of an inherently unstable world, playing a role difficult to reconcile with some of Christianity's core messages.

Yet, the one thing the church had going for it was the promise of redemptive unity, which however imperfectly manifested today, was always something one could conceptualize as possible for tomorrow. How to get there was the question. There were those like Luther who broke with Catholic theology, believing that since human beings were so small, so finite, when compared to an infinite god, that nothing they could do in life could help them be saved. "Good works" were things that human beings should strive to do but not because they could help one earn salvation. Salvation was up to no one but God,

so that it was by faith alone, which one understood by scripture alone, that one could ready oneself for God's saving grace,
something he would freely give if—and only if—he so chose.
This Lutheran position ultimately does away with a motivated
free will in a strict, philosophical sense. If God is omnipotent
and omniscient, there is nothing you can do that he could not
have foreseen, and in any case whatever you do will not earn
you salvation or condemnation, since that decision is up to God
alone. There were others, like a host of Catholic reformers, who
believed in preserving human free will, not just as a power of
choice in individual discrete actions but as something that could
help one earn God's grace, not in a guaranteed fashion but
working together with God ("cooperating" with God, in theological terms) as a partner, a junior one to be sure but a partner
nonetheless. One can go down many a dark and winding rabbit
hole, theologically and philosophically speaking, attempting to
reconcile the two fundamentally incompatible positions.

And then there were those like Machiavelli, who didn't care
about theology but who felt that contemporary Christianity
was not helping things in political terms. In his case, as we have
seen, the papacy was problematic because, to protect itself
and its territorial claims, it had a tradition of bringing foreign
powers into Italy. Christianity as such—as religion pure and
simple—was blameworthy since it exalted humility, when a
proper religion (meaning for Machiavelli one whose rituals and
assumptions strengthened a citizenry) would instead lead to a
desire on the part of citizens for worldly glory.

Here the key word is "ritual." On the one hand, for thinking
people—and Machiavelli was certainly one of those—religion
is about ideas, represented as theology and as philosophy. On

the other, for everyone, thinkers included, religion is even more strongly about ritual: regular, repeated behaviors that themselves lead to those most powerful but, importantly, unarticulated assumptions—those things we believe without really knowing consciously that we believe them. You simply could not be raised in Renaissance Christian culture without having the idea drummed into you that there was a salvation-oriented ideal available.

The intellectual side of Machiavelli could indeed criticize not only the church, as many anti-clerical Italians did from Boccaccio onward, but also the central messages of Christianity itself. This was Machiavelli the active man who had repeatedly seen the best laid plans of men ruined by fortune, who read Lucretius so attentively that he hand-copied that thinker's repeated message of a cold universe whose god, unsympathetic to human beings, ruled all from a perch inaccessible and remote. This was the Machiavelli whose cynicism only grew more marked and severe, the more that he saw that even those perceived to be highly religious were human, all too human. But intellectuals, no matter how self-aware (and self-awareness was not among Machiavelli's many virtues), carry around assumptions that they may not know they possess, forged in childhood, based on repeated behaviors.

Here we are talking about Machiavelli the boy, who every week and on many holy days would have seen a priest, majestic and mysterious, with his back toward the congregation, performing a miracle in Latin, a language made sacred on the cross, as he raised the host and transformed it into the body of Christ. Machiavelli would have seen altarpieces and other paintings representing the crucifixion and been told, "You see, Niccolò, that man, who was both man and god, died for us, for our sins, and someday he will come back to save us all." His ritualistic experiences of Christianity would have convinced him beyond unconvincing that the possibility of an ideal existed. If in Machiavelli's mind he was able to move away from a contemporary Christian ideal of salvation, in his heart he approached it nonetheless when it came to Italy, as the ideal prince or ideal republic hovered spectrally above his thought, something that with writerly discipline he could often suppress but never entirely, as one sees in the last, hortatory chapter of *The Prince*, or in the *Discourses*, with their idealized Roman republic, or at the end of the *Art of War*.

Salvific religion or salvific politics—either way we cannot see real evidence of these things in our life. But we can dream, as did Machiavelli, who was one of those rare dreamers so incisive, passionate, and clear, that he provided succeeding generations with thoughts on which other intellectual edifices might be built. And this is the final ghost that haunts Machiavelli: the ghost of interpretation. The great twentieth-century thinker Isaiah Berlin remarked, in a classic essay on Machiavelli, how striking it was that, for a thinker universally praised for his clarity, interpretations of Machiavelli varied so greatly. Berlin presented a lengthy résumé of opinions on Machiavelli from the sixteenth century up to his own day (he was writing in 1972), a tour de force, really, turning the bibliographic essay into an art form.[4] Were he writing today, he would have still more material on which to report, and the diversity of opinion would be just as marked as before, if not more so.

The primary reason for this diversity has to do, needless to say, with the predilections of interpreters. Those who have wished to see a theorist of absolutism can find material in Machiavelli. So can those who wish to see a theorist of republicanism. Yet that word, "theorist," puts the cart before the horse by a few centuries, as it implies a thinker reaching for systematic coherence in his thought, an impulse that is not strongly present in Machiavelli. True, he will in one work refer to another, in his letters we can find things that seem to harmonize with some of his writings, and his thinking does possess a unity of style: conversational and dialogue-like. But that is about as far as you can go if you stick to his texts. The only underlying significant commonality to be found is the absolute necessity, for any state—princedom or republic—to put military matters first. It is out of this core notion that everything else radiates: the way rulers and governments wield power (no matter how clever they may be, they must first and foremost have a monopoly of force to be effective), the way a well-functioning religion should work (in a martial fashion, as did ancient Roman religion in Machiavelli's view, with awe-inspiring ceremonies and bloody sacrifices that made men ferocious and on the hunt for worldly glory), and the way ideal citizens should comport themselves (winning battles for their homeland and thus acquiring an inherent political legitimacy). Most modern interpreters have not engaged in military conflict, and all are far removed from the on-the-doorstep realities of the yearly military campaigns that were a regular feature of life in Machiavelli's day. For these reasons, modern interpreters have focused, understandably, on seeing whether one might draw some consistent political messages out of Machiavelli by interpreting what he wrote.

Not that there is anything wrong with interpretation. As we have seen, Machiavelli was a great interpreter, of the ancient historian Livy in particular. When it came to Livy, though, Machiavelli was not trying to find a unitary truth present in Livy's work. He was instead reading Livy carefully to see how the lessons contained in Livy's work could benefit contemporary society—its politics, culture, and even religion. Like all great works, those of Machiavelli should be treated in a similar fashion: as historical sources, to be sure, but also as founts of inspiration. If he is clear enough on what he means—military matters come first, observe the present carefully, and take lessons, when appropriate, from the past—his messages still demand reinterpretation as times change and as different contexts present themselves. Without making the mistake of imposing thoroughly modern theoretical frameworks on Machiavelli, we can still isolate at least three ways in which his thought is not only relevant, but even essential, today.

First, his ideas on the presence and inevitability of conflict deserve attention. Machiavelli says that even in well-ordered states there will inevitably be conflict, as different groups vie for their share of the pie. This notion is worth keeping in mind whenever politicians promise universal solutions, whether through offering a different style of governing, running against the system, or avowing conciliation among steadfast rivals. Despite his occasional rhetorical forays into salvific mode (the possibility of an ideal prince or ideal republic), the message we should draw from Machiavelli is that real leadership demands an acceptance of the inevitability of conflict and a determination to manage it effectively.

He did not put it this way, but institution building represents the core message here. For example, in his *Discourses* Machiavelli asserts that conflict between men of the senatorial class and those of the "plebs" actually helped Rome grow strong from the fifth to the first centuries BC (members of the "plebs," here the terms "plebeians" or "commoners," mean those who were not of senatorial, "old families" but who nonetheless held property and believed they were entitled to a share of power). Military matters come first, of course, as Machiavelli acknowledges that both fortune and the military contributed to Rome's success and growth. But normally, "where there is a good military, there is usually also good order, and it only rarely happens that there is not also good fortune."[5] Reading Livy's account of those (roughly) four centuries, one finds numerous instances of discord: "the people yelling at the Senate, the Senate doing the same in return, people running tumultuously through the streets, shops being closed down," and so on, all of which, Machiavelli admits, can cause unease in a reader.[6] But Machiavelli believes all of this was beneficial in the end.

The people always need opportunities to blow off steam, he suggests, and in any case "the desires of free peoples are rarely harmful to liberty, since they stem either from being oppressed or from the belief that they have been oppressed."[7] If they have been truly oppressed, these occasions of tumult offer the opportunity for redress. And if not, public assemblies can help convince the people that their fears were unfounded, since a good orator can help correct misunderstandings. Machiavelli alludes to a commonplace drawn from antiquity, to the effect that "even if the people may be unlearned, they are capable of grasping the truth, provided a trustworthy man presents them with what is true."[8] What Machiavelli, and indeed what the ancients, had in mind here, was the classic definition of the perfect orator, as someone who was a *vir bonus dicendi peritus*—a "good man well skilled in the art of communicating."[9]

This is a thinker, Machiavelli, from over five hundred years ago, commenting on a text, Livy's *History*, written almost fifteen hundred years before he was born. How can these recondite examples, shrouded in the mists of ancient history, help us today? Most of all, one might argue, through the faith Machiavelli puts in the idea of the public at large to function within an institutional system in which people have maintained at least some trust. It is this trust that is lacking today. We have seen over the last two decades the rise of what is called, evocatively in modern Italian, *antipolitica*, "antipolitics." The term is used to signal the belief that politics—in every possible manifestation—must be corrupt. Machiavelli, despite all evidence to the contrary in his own experience, continued to believe, perhaps even to dream, that a viable politics could exist, one that could not eliminate conflict among people but could mitigate it, satisfying different constituencies in a way that was necessarily imperfect but at least not hopeless.

We can also jump beyond Machiavelli's texts, as he himself often did with Livy and other authors he read, to see where his thought gets us today. Machiavelli could never have begun to dream of the media world in which we live. In his day, printing with moveable type had only been around for a half century, and he functioned, for the works he deemed most important, as if he lived in the old world of manuscripts, circulating handwritten copies of his works to a relatively small circle of intimates. But in a turn of fate that Machiavelli would have loved, given how much he appreciated cyclical theories of history, we have returned in many ways to a pre-modern media landscape, when it comes to how we read and write.

The key is how "local" things were in Machiavelli's day and how they have become so once again. The great media transformation we are undergoing—certainly more far-reaching and faster than the change to printing with movable type—was heralded at its outset as a transformative vehicle: the Internet was expected to democratize reading and writing, offering publishing platforms to countless people who might otherwise have been excluded from publishing their ideas. To a large extent this transformation has occurred and even continues to intensify, with newer modes of delivery sparking new uses. Twitter allowed instantaneous broadcasting of transformative revolutions in the Middle East, for example, that both traditional journalism as well as repressive home state media regimes would not have permitted. There has been an efflorescence of excellent essay writing, with "long-form" journalism coming into its own as new outlets have emerged and as online presences of traditional publications have permitted their reach to widen.

There has been a cost to all of this change in the media landscape, as well. First, there is the bottom line. No one needs to be reminded of the parlous state of the newspaper industry, which for decades relied on classified advertising as a significant income stream, something that services like Craigslist and Angie's List have essentially made obsolete. Failing to be able to make up that missing revenue from other sources, numerous US newspapers have closed or radically reduced their staff and reportage, from New Orleans (the *Times-Picayune*) to Seattle (the *Post-Intelligencer*), to Denver (the *Rocky Mountain News*). And venerable newspapers and journals—like the *Washington*

Post and *The New Republic*, to cite two examples—have had to be "adopted" by patrons whose pockets are deep enough that the publications in question do not need to worry about making significant profits in the short and medium term.

How does all of this relate to Machiavelli? In a society like that of the contemporary United States and many other Western democracies, our media world represents one key constituent part of the public square Machiavelli foreshadowed. When he says, in our example above, that people need a chance to voice their opinions, even their grievances, he could just as well be talking about the complex, ever-shifting ecosystem represented by the vast social media landscape with which all of us are surrounded. We don't have small public assemblies anymore, when it comes to politics at the national level. Instead, we have this broad, interlocking set of public forums, still new enough that no underlying norms of civility and transparency have developed.

More importantly, Machiavelli also calls—in his language, not in ours—for a beneficial combination of transparency and service, when he argues that people, no matter their level of education, can apprehend the truth if it is presented with integrity. If it was inevitable in a small, essentially face-to-face culture, to reckon with the fact that groups of citizens will feel aggrieved—sometimes rightly, sometimes wrongly—how much more so is it necessary to recognize this truth now? After all, the numbers of participants in democratic society have skyrocketed, even as many feel that their government is almost impossibly distant.

There are two key ingredients that can help ameliorate, if never eliminate, this problem: a media culture that fosters transparency in institutions and an institutional culture of explanation, whereby those charged with serving the public perceive a need to explain what they are doing at least as far as possible. In the best of all possible worlds, these two impulses would work together. But we do not live in the best of all possible worlds. Increasingly, citizens are living divided, separate existences, and even media-savvy political junkies tend more and more to pick and choose among media outlets until they find the ones that agree with their intuitive perceptions. It is hard to have a common conversation, in other words.

Machiavelli's unsystematic but brilliant intuitions can serve as an inspiration to improve. Not to perfect anything, because perfection is not our lot in life, but to get better: to keep trying to make our institutions better, to look at them from without, as good journalists must do, but also to serve them from within. Machiavelli, this willful, brilliant, impatient thinker, with all his flaws and humanity, kept trying to serve his institutions and, when he couldn't, to write about the possibility of improving them. Knowing that he did so in the full belief that there would always be conflict, that perfect peace and tranquility could never be achieved, should remind us, young and old alike, how meaningful this ideal of service can be. This notion, that service should be undertaken without the promise of a utopian future, points to the second of Machiavelli's enduring lessons, which has to do with leadership.

Countless writers have drawn lessons for leadership from Machiavelli, but it is a theme so important that it is worth examining in light of current realities. Three passages in Machiavelli's work come to the fore. The first occurs in chapter three of Machiavelli's *Prince*. There he is considering the complicated issue of what he calls "mixed" princedoms, usually meaning when a new state is joined to an old one (as when France briefly held Milan or when the Turks more perdurably occupied and held Byzantium). As always, he has cases to examine and examples to emulate. Of the latter it will come as no surprise that none is more important than that of the ancient Romans, who were wise enough, Machiavelli says, to establish colonies in lands they wanted to annex to their own. This was a good move, "because in these cases the Romans did what all wise princes ought to do, which is that they shouldn't consider only current problems but also future ones and make all effort to head them off at the pass. The reason is that, seeing problems at a distance, one resolves them with ease, whereas if one waits until they are upon one, the medicine doesn't arrive in time, since the disease is incurable."[10] Three sentences later, Machiavelli writes: "The Romans, seeing potential problems from far off, always remedied them and never let them come to fruition just to flee a war, because they knew that war is never avoided, just postponed, to the advantage of others."[11]

This section of *The Prince* can be paired with another passage, from the *Florentine Histories,* where Machiavelli discusses Cosimo de' Medici. For all Machiavelli's ambivalence toward the Medici, he did recognize that Cosimo was a special type of leader and a special type of person: "in the midst of such a variety of fortune and such an unstable citizenry, he held on to a state for thirty-one years, and because he was so very prudent, he recognized evils at a distance."[12]

The final passage comes from Machiavelli's *Discourses:* Moses "had to kill countless men in order to realize his laws and plans, men who were motivated to oppose his designs by nothing other than jealous hatred."[13]

When it comes to leadership, what all these passages have in common is the future, as they emphasize that successful leaders look as much, or more, to the future, as they do to the immediate present. The passages also have more to tell us. First, as to the Romans, yet again we see that Machiavelli's political thought is not divided between republics and princedoms. Both can be governed well or poorly, and in this case the ancient Romans in their republican period provided an example that princes could emulate: looking toward the future and addressing potential problems early. To a certain extent Cosimo de' Medici did just that, though as we have seen Machiavelli's feelings about him are ambivalent, since Cosimo in many ways acted like a prince without actually officially changing Florence's republican form of government. Most noteworthy, however, are Machiavelli's unsurprising (by now) references to war and to the need to do things that might seem distasteful. Yet again, we are reminded that for Machiavelli military matters came first.

To draw lessons for contemporary leadership of all sorts from these comments, we can say that leadership involves recognizing conflict and competition and managing them, and cultivating the ability to do things for the good of the institution one is serving that are difficult and often unsavory: firing a long-time colleague, say, who has not kept up with evolving standards; not hiring a good friend, who though close to you is not the best candidate for the position; or, on the larger geopolitical level, making calculations and consequent decisions that may seem unpalatable at present but will hopefully secure a better future. In all those cases, absolute certainty of outcomes is not possible, and it falls to the person in a leadership position to make decisions that, though controversial, are also necessary.

Through everything Machiavelli writes, leadership included, it is the concern for the future that he privileges. We see this concern not only in the passages above, but also in his distinction, in the *Florentine Histories*, between the ways in which a citizen can gain esteem through means either "public" (service-oriented) or "private" (doing favors for friends, and so on). The preferable type of citizen was the one who gained esteem through public means. And we can recall from the *Discourses* his praise for Rome's second king, Numa, who instituted Roman religious practices and thereby gave ancient Rome an institutional culture that went beyond his own rule. Thereafter Machiavelli remarked: "So it happens that those reigns that depend principally on the virtue of one man do not last, since that virtue disappears when he does . . . therefore it is not conducive to the health of a republic or a kingdom to have a prince who governs prudently while he lives, but rather to have one who orders things in such a way that the health of the republic or kingdom is preserved even when he dies."[14] Why did Machiavelli care so much about styles of leadership that looked toward the future? Perhaps it was because he saw the evanescence of the republic he had served and sensed its inexorable march toward one-man rule. Perhaps his concern for the future arose from his study of ancient texts, from which he selected what was best, institutionally speaking, and then found ways to highlight those things in a manner that his many later readers found useful and stimulating (so much so that one can draw a line, as some critics have done, from Machiavelli's various hints and suggestions in his works, to the American founders).[15]

And yet, his hints and suggestions are just those things. Far from offering systematic theories, Machiavelli presents a vast treasury of possible positions through which run certain lines of continuity, lines whose relations to each other will necessarily alter over time as conditions and contexts change. In so doing he urges us to read him the way he read the past: in an interpretive, creative fashion. It is up to us to choose.

◆ ◆ ◆

So in the end, how should we view Machiavelli? Other than his military triumph in Pisa in 1509, most of what he suggested did not come to fruition in his own life. He seems after his period of public life (1498–1512) to have just missed the boat, coming close but never close enough to reading the political moment surrounding him. To understand Machiavelli, we should listen to how he signs off on one of his letters, to his great friend Francesco Guicciardini, in 1525, where Machiavelli refers to himself as: *historico, comico, et tragico.*[16] One way to translate this phrase would be as "historian, comic writer, and tragic writer." But of course Machiavelli did not write tragedies. He experienced them. That was what he was referring to with the last word, *tragico.*

As to the second word, *comico* (to go in reverse order), like the other two it is an adjective, modifying Machiavelli. He is writing in that letter *as* a writer and of course he wrote successful comedies, as we have seen. So it is reasonable, and on the surface correct, to infer the meaning "comic author." Yet the word has a broader significance, pointing as much to a view of life as to a genre of professional activity. What Machiavelli means is that, yes, serious matters exist and are, in the end, the most important. For Machiavelli these were, primarily, military wisdom, participation in politics, and diplomatic activity. Each of us will have his or her own matters that are the most serious, the things we believe intuitively are most meaningful and that make the world a better place. But Machiavelli the *comico* reminds us to have the courage, confidence, and poise not to take ourselves too seriously, to remember that the world will continue to turn without us, and to understand that sometimes the best thing we can do for ourselves, our friends, and our community, is to step back and laugh.

To end with the first and most important word, *historico*, what Machiavelli means is quite clear. History shaped his internal life and mental outlook profoundly. He lived history in the first part of his career, as a front-line witness to wars and diplomatic dealings, a shaper of policy, and as a key office-holder in a major city-state. The second part of his career included deep engagement with written history, as he took his own experiences and combined them with the insights, narratives, and manifold theories that he drew out of Livy and other ancient landmark texts. *The Prince*, the *Discourses*, the *Art of War*, and the *Florentine Histories*: these major works all emerged as products of Machiavelli's dual trajectory as a political actor and as a writer. Finally—and this the third and last lesson we can draw from him—Machiavelli never stopped trying to be involved, never stopped trying to serve, no matter how dire the circumstances seemed. This Machiavelli was, to use his own expression, Machiavelli *historico*, a person subject to and involved in history, who believed, however improbably, that by interpreting the past sagely, one could act more fruitfully in the present.

Notes

1. Renaissance, Conspiracies, Bonfires

1. Bernardo Machiavelli, *Ricordi*, ed. Leonardo Olschki (Florence: Le Monnier, 1954).

2. See Daniel Hobbins, *Authorship and Publicity before Print: Jean Gerson and the Transformation of Late Medieval Learning* (Philadelphia: University of Pennsylvania Press, 2009).

3. Francesco Petrarca (Petrarch), *Le familiari / Rerum familiarum libri*, ed. Vittorio Rossi, 4 vols. (Florence: Le Lettere, 1997), 22.2.

4. Ibid., 24.3.

5. Dante, *Inferno*, 4.131.

6. See Christopher S. Celenza, "End Game: Humanist Latin in the Late Fifteenth Century," in Y. Maes, J. Papy, and W. Verbaal, eds., *Latinitas Perennis II: Appropriation and Latin Literature* (Leiden: Brill, 2009), 201–242.

7. Quintilian, *Institutio oratoria*, 1.1.4.

8. Jacob Burckhardt, *Die Cultur der Renaissance in Italien: Ein Versuch* (Basel: Schweighauser, 1860), 131; Burckhardt, *The Civilisation of the Renaissance in Italy*, trans. S. C. J. Middlemore (London: Kegan Paul and Co., 1878), 100.

9. For bibliography on this point, see Mikael Hörnquist, "The Two Myths of Civic Humanism," in James Hankins, ed., *Renaissance Civic Humanism: Reappraisals and Reflections* (Cambridge: Cambridge University Press, 2000), 105–142.

10. Angelo Poliziano, "Commentary on the Pazzi Conspiracy," trans. Elizabeth B. Welles, in Benjamin Kohl and Ronald G. Witt, eds., *The*

Earthly Republic (Philadelphia: University of Pennsylvania Press, 1978), 305–324, at 313.

11. Ibid., 314–316.

12. Ibid., 319–320.

13. Ibid., 321.

14. On conspiracies in the Renaissance, see Anthony F. D'Elia, *A Sudden Terror: The Plot to Murder the Pope in Renaissance Rome* (Cambridge, Mass.: Harvard University Press, 2009).

15. Lorenzo de' Medici, *Canti carnascialeschi*, ed. Paolo Orvieto (Rome: Salerno editrice, 1991), 80.

16. Among many studies, see F. William Kent, *Lorenzo de' Medici and the Art of Magnificence* (Baltimore: Johns Hopkins University Press, 2004).

17. See L. Martines, *Fire in the City: Savonarola and the Struggle for the Soul of Florence* (Oxford: Oxford University Press, 2006); and Donald Weinstein, *Savonarola: The Rise and Fall of a Renaissance Prophet* (New Haven, Conn.: Yale University Press, 2011).

2. Highs and Lows

1. Niccolò Machiavelli, *Opere*, 3 vols., ed. Corrado Vivanti (Turin: Einaudi-Galimard, 1997–2005), 2.676.

2. Ibid., 2.790–791.

3. Ibid., 2.757.

4. Ibid., 1.104–105.

5. David Bell, *The First Total War: Napoleon's Europe and the Birth of Warfare as We Know It* (New York: Houghton Mifflin, 2007). Though the idea of perpetual peace after major wars is present in the biblical and apocalyptic traditions, the notion that a human-instituted perpetual peace was conceivable is traceable, as Bell shows, to the Enlightenment.

6. Machiavelli, *Opere*, 1.107.

7. Roslyn Pesman Cooper, "Machiavelli, Francesco Soderini, and don Michelotto," *Nuova rivista storica* 66 (1982): 342–357.

8. Carrie Benes, *Urban Legends: Civic Identity and the Classical Past in Northern Italy, 1250–1350* (State College: Pennsylvania State University Press, 2011).

9. Virgil, *Aeneid*, 6.853–854, in *P. Vergili Maronis Opera*, ed. R. A. B. Mynors (Oxford: Oxford University Press, 1969).

10. Livy, *Ab urbe condita*, books 6–10, ed. R. S. Conway and C. F. Walters (Oxford: Oxford University Press, 1963), 8.13.

11. Ibid.

12. Machiavelli, *Opere*, 1.24.

13. Ibid.

14. *Pratica*, in Denis Fachard, ed., *Consulte e pratiche della Repubblica fiorentina, 1505–1512* (Geneva: Droz, 1988), 77, cited in Mikael Hörnquist, "Perché non si usa allegare i Romani: Machiavelli and the Florentine Militia of 1506," *Renaissance Quarterly* 55 (2002): 148–191, at 166n86.

15. Machiavelli, *Opere*, 1.27.

16. Ibid., 1.28.

17. Ibid., 1.29.

18. Ibid., 1.507; see also Hörnquist, "Perché non si usa allegare i Romani," 172.

19. Luca Landucci, *Diario fiorentino dal 1450 al 1516* (Florence: Biblos, 1969), 273; Hörnquist, "Perché non si usa allegare i Romani," 156n33.

20. Bartolomeo Cerretani, *Storia fiorentina*, ed. G. Berti (Florence: Olschki, 1994), 347; Hörnquist, "Perché non si usa allegare i Romani," 160n57.

21. It has been suggested that Machiavelli worked on this plan alongside Leonardo da Vinci; see R. D. Masters, *Fortune Is a River: Leonardo da Vinci and Machiavelli's Magnificent Dream to Change the Course of Florentine History* (New York: Free Press, 1998). However, there is no solid documentary evidence that the two collaborated. At most what one can say is they might have met and discussed plans for the river.

22. Hörnquist, "Perché non si usa allegare i Romani," 162n65.

23. Machiavelli, *Opere*, 2.188.

24. Ibid., 2.234–235.

25. Ibid., 1.87–188.

26. This document was discovered recently by Stephen J. Milner and published in his "'Fanno bandire, notificare, et expressamente comandare': Town Criers and the Information Economy of Renaissance Florence," *I Tatti Studies in the Italian Renaissance* 16 (2013): 107–151, at 150.

27. Machiavelli, *Opere*, 2.235–236.

28. Ibid., 2.241.

29. Ibid., 2.287, 2.290.

3. *Interlude*

1. Niccolò Machiavelli, *Opere,* 3 vols., ed. Corrado Vivanti (Turin: Einaudi-Galimard, 1997–2005), 2.294–297.

2. Aulus Gellius, *Noctes atticae,* ed. P. K. Marshall (Oxford: Oxford University Press, 1990), 13.17.

3. Dante Alighieri, *Comedia,* ed. Federico Sanguineti (Florence: Edizioni del Galluzzo, 2001), *Paradiso,* 5.41–42.

4. The Prince

1. Francis Bacon, *The Advancement of Learning,* ed. William A. Wright (Oxford: Clarendon, 1880), 2.21.9.

2. Niccolò Machiavelli, *Opere,* 3 vols., ed. Corrado Vivanti (Turin: Einaudi-Galimard, 1997–2005), 1.117.

3. *Discourses,* 3.43, in *Opere,* 1.517.

4. Cristoforo Landino, "Orazione fatta per Cristofano da Pratovecchio quando cominciò a leggere i sonnetti di messer Francesco Petrarca in istudio," in Roberto Cardini, *La critica del Landino* (Florence: Sansoni, 1973), 342–354, at 350.

5. Poggio Bracciolini, *On Avarice,* trans. Benjamin Kohl and Elizabeth B. Welles, in Benjamin Kohl and Ronald G. Witt, eds., *The Earthly Republic* (Philadelphia: University of Pennsylvania Press, 1978), 241–289.

6. Lapo da Castiglionchio the Younger, "On the Benefits of the Papal Court," in Christopher S. Celenza, *Renaissance Humanism and the Papal Curia: Lapo da Castiglionchio the Younger's* De curiae commodis (Ann Arbor: University of Michigan Press, 1999), 102–227.

7. *Prince,* 7, in *Opere,* 1.138.

8. *Prince,* 3, in *Opere,* 1.122.

9. *Prince,* preface, in *Opere,* 1.117–118.

10. *Prince,* preface, in *Opere,* 1.118.

11. *Prince,* 15, in *Opere,* 1.159.

12. Ibid.

13. Ibid.

14. Ibid.

15. Ibid.

16. Ibid.

17. *Prince*, 18, in *Opere*, 1.165.

18. *Prince*, 18, in *Opere*, 1.166.

19. Ibid.

20. Ibid.

21. *Prince*, 6, in *Opere*, 1.130.

22. *Prince*, 14, in *Opere*, 1.158.

23. *Prince*, 25, in *Opere*, 1.186.

24. *Prince*, 25, in *Opere*, 1.186–187.

25. *Prince*, 25, in *Opere*, 1.187.

26. *Prince*, 11, in *Opere*, 1.147–148.

27. *Prince*, 11, in *Opere*, 1.148.

28. *Prince*, 6, in *Opere*, 1.131.

29. Ibid.

30. Ibid.

31. Ibid.

32. *Prince*, 25, in *Opere*, 1.187.

33. Ibid., for last three citations.

34. *Prince*, 25, in *Opere*, 1.187–188.

35. *Prince*, 25, in *Opere*, 1.188.

36. Ibid.

37. Ibid.

38. *Prince*, 25, in *Opere*, 1.189.

39. Ibid.

40. *Prince*, 12, in *Opere*, 1.150.

41. Ibid.

42. *Prince*, 12, in *Opere*, 1.151.

43. *Prince*, 13, in *Opere*, 1.154.

44. Ibid.

45. Ibid.

46. *Prince*, 13, in *Opere*, 1.156; cf. Tacitus, *Annalium ab excessu divi Augusti libri*, ed. Charles D. Fisher (Oxford: Oxford University Press, 1906), 13.19.

47. Sydney Anglo, *Machiavelli: The First Century* (Oxford: Oxford University Press, 2005).

48. *Prince*, 3, in *Opere*, 1.124, 1.126.

49. *Prince*, 14, in *Opere*, 1.157.

50. Ibid.

51. Ibid.

52. *Prince*, 14, in *Opere*, 1.158.

53. *Prince*, 14, in *Opere*, 1.159.

54. *Prince*, 16, in *Opere*, 1.160–162.

55. *Prince*, 17, in *Opere*, 1.162–164.

56. *Prince*, 7, in *Opere*, 1.136–137. The "piece of wood" refers to the block on which the head is placed before being severed.

57. *Prince*, 8, in *Opere*, 1.140.

58. Ibid.

59. *Prince*, 17, in *Opere*, 1.163.

60. Ibid.

61. Ibid.

62. Ibid.

63. Ibid.

64. Aristotle, *Politica*, ed. David Ross (Oxford: Oxford University Press, 1957), 1311a, Machiavelli, *Discourses*, 3.26, in *Opere*, 1.485.

65. Letter to Giovanni de' Medici, future Pope Leo X, October 1512, cited in Machiavelli, *Il Principe*, ed. Giorgio Inglese (Turin: Einaudi, 1995), 112.

66. *Prince*, 17, in *Opere*, 1.164.

67. Ibid.

68. *Prince*, 20, in *Opere*, 1.175–176.

69. *Prince*, 20, in *Opere*, 1.178.

70. Ibid.

71. Ibid.

72. *Prince*, 20, in *Opere*, 1.179.

73. *Prince*, 21, in *Opere*, 1.180.

74. Ibid.

75. *Prince*, 22, in *Opere*, 1.182–183.

76. *Prince*, 23, in *Opere*, 1.183–185.

77. *Prince*, 24, in *Opere*, 1.185–186.

78. Petrarca, *Canzoniere*, 128.

79. The theme of the "redeemer prince" is stressed in Maurizio Viroli, *Redeeming* The Prince: *The Meaning of Machiavelli's Masterpiece* (Princeton, N.J.: Princeton University Press, 2013).

80. *Prince*, 26, in *Opere*, 1.192.

81. *Prince*, 9, in *Opere*, 1.143–146.

82. *Prince*, 9, in *Opere*, 1.143.

5. Conversing with the Ancients

1. Pliny the Younger, *Epistularum libri decem*, ed. Roger Mynors (Oxford: Oxford University Press, 1963), 2.3.

2. G. Billanovich, *La tradizione del testo di Livio e le origini dell'umanesimo*, 2 vols. (Padua: Antenore, 1981).

3. J. H. Whitfield, "Machiavelli's Use of Livy," in T. A. Dorey, ed., *Livy* (London: Routledge, 1971), 73–96, at 74, citing Bernardo Machiavelli, *Libro di ricordi*, 35, 223.

4. Livy, *Ab urbe condita*, books 1–5, ed. Robert M. Ogilvie (Oxford: Oxford University Press, 1974), Praefatio.6.

5. Ibid., Praefatio.7.

6. Ibid., Praefatio.7–8.

7. Ibid., Praefatio.8–9.

8. Ibid., Praefatio.9.

9. Ibid., Praefatio.10.

10. Ibid., 3.34.

11. *Discourses*, 1.40, in Niccolò Machiavelli, *Opere*, 3 vols., ed. Corrado Vivanti (Turin: Einaudi-Galimard, 1997–2005), 1.284.

12. Livy, *Ab urbe condita*, 3.36.

13. Ibid., 3.38.

14. Ibid.

15. Ibid., 3.41.

16. Ibid., 3.44.

17. Ibid.

18. Ibid.

19. Ibid., 3.47.

20. Ibid.

21. Ibid., 3.48.

22. Ibid.

23. Ibid.

24. Ibid., 3.50.

25. Ibid.

26. Ibid., 3.54.

27. Ibid., 3.55.

28. Ibid., 3.58.

29. *Discourses*, 1.40, in *Opere*, 1.286.

30. *Prince*, 2, in *Opere*, 1.119.

31. *Discourses*, 2.2, in *Opere*, 1.331.

32. *Discourses*, 2.proemio, in *Opere*, 1.324.

33. *Discourses*, 2.proemio, in *Opere*, 1.325.

34. *Discourses*, 2.proemio, in *Opere*, 1.326.

35. Ibid.

36. Ibid.

37. *Discourses*, 2.proemio, in *Opere*, 1.327.

38. Ibid.

39. Ibid.

40. See the treatment in Patricia J. Osmond, "The Conspiracy of 1522 against Cardinal Giulio de' Medici: Machiavelli and *gli esempli degli antiqui*," in K. Gouwens and S. E. Reiss, eds., *The Pontificate of Clement VII: Politics, History, Culture* (Aldershot: Ashgate, 2005), 55–72.

41. Filippo de' Nerli, *Commentari de' fatti civili occursi dentro la città di Firenze dall'anno 1215 al 1537* (Augsburg: Mertz and Mayer, 1728), 138.

42. Letter in *Opere*, 2.371.

43. See John Najemy, "Introduction," in John M. Najemy, ed., *The Cambridge Companion to Machiavelli* (Cambridge: Cambridge University Press, 2010), 2–4.

44. *Discourses*, 1.11, in *Opere*, 1.229.

45. Ibid.

46. Ibid.

47. *Discourses*, 1.11, in *Opere*, 1.231.

48. Ibid.

49. Ibid.

50. Ibid.

51. *Discourses*, 1.12, in *Opere*, 1.233.

52. Ibid.
53. Ibid.
54. Ibid.
55. Ibid.
56. *Discourses*, 1.12, in *Opere*, 1.234.
57. Ibid.
58. *Discourses*, 2.2, in *Opere*, 1.333.
59. Ibid.
60. *Ibid.*
61. Ibid.
62. *Discourses*, 2.2, in *Opere*, 1.333–334.
63. Ibid., 1.334.

6. The Comedy of Life

1. *Genesis* 30 and in the *Song of Songs*, 7.
2. *Mandragola*, in Niccolò Machiavelli, *Opere*, 3 vols., ed. Corrado Vivanti (Turin: Einaudi-Galimard, 1997–2005), 3.145.
3. Ibid., 3.173.
4. Ibid., 3.184.
5. Ibid., 3.185.
6. MS Vatican City, Biblioteca Apostolica Vaticana, Rossi 884. See Sergio Bertelli and Franco Gaeta, "Noterelle Machiavelliane: Un codice di Lucrezio e di Terenzio," *Rivista storica italiana* 73 (1961): 544–555; Chauncey E. Finch, "Machiavelli's Copy of Lucretius," *Classical Journal* 56 (1960): 29–32.
7. For Lucretius in the Renaissance see Alison Brown, *The Return of Lucretius to Renaissance Florence* (Cambridge, Mass.: Harvard University Press, 2010); Stephen Greenblatt, *The Swerve: How the World Became Modern* (New York: Norton, 2012); Gerard Passanante, *The Lucretian Renaissance: Philology and the Afterlife of Tradition* (Chicago: University of Chicago Press, 2011); and Ada Palmer, *Reading Lucretius in the Renaissance* (Cambridge, Mass.: Harvard University Press, 2014).
8. Lucretius, *De Rerum Natura*, ed. Cyril Bailey (Oxford: Oxford University Press, 1922), 2.83.

9. See Christopher S. Celenza, "Late Antiquity and the Italian Renaissance," in S. F. Johnson, ed., *The Oxford Handbook of Late Antiquity* (Oxford: Oxford University Press, 2012), 1172–1199.

10. *Mandragola*, in *Opere*, 3.144.

11. Letter of Marietta, November 24, 1503, in *Opere*, 2.93.

12. Letter of Biagio Buonaccorsi, December 4, 1503, in *Opere*, 2.95.

13. Letter of Biagio Buonaccorsi, December 21, 1502, in *Opere*, 2.77.

14. Letter of Biagio Buonaccorsi, December 22, 1502, in *Opere*, 2.78.

15. Letter of Biagio Buonaccorsi, November 2, 1503, in *Opere*, 2.84.

16. Letter of Luca Ugolini, November 11, 1503, in *Opere*, 2.86.

17. Letter of Biagio Buonaccorsi, November 15, 1503, in *Opere*, 2.88.

18. Letter of Biagio Buonaccorsi, November 17, 1503, in *Opere*, 2.90.

19. Letter of Machiavelli, April 11, 1527, in *Opere*, 2.456.

20. Letter of Roberto Acciauoli, October 7, 1510, in *Opere*, 2.224.

21. Letter of Machiavelli, December 19, 1513, in *Opere*, 2.299–300.

22. *Opere*, 2.1587n1, cited in Guido Ruggiero, *Machiavelli in Love: Sex, Self, and Society in the Italian Renaissance* (Baltimore: Johns Hopkins University Press, 2007), 129.

23. A fine analysis of their correspondence is John M. Najemy, *Between Friends: Discourses of Power and Desire in the Machiavelli-Vettori Letters of 1513–1515* (Princeton, N.J.: Princeton University Press, 1993).

24. Letter of Francesco Vettori, December 24, 1513, in *Opere*, 2.300.

25. Ibid., 2.301.

26. Ibid.

27. Ibid.

28. Ibid., 2.302.

29. Ibid.

30. Letter of Machiavelli, January 5, 1514, in *Opere*, 3.303.

31. Ibid., 3.304.

32. *Opere*, 2.386, cited in Michael Rocke, *Forbidden Friendships: Homosexuality and Male Culture in Renaissance Florence* (Oxford: Oxford University Press, 1996), 114.

33. See Rocke, *Forbidden Friendships*.

34. Letter of Vettori, January 1514, in *Opere*, 2.307–308.

35. Ibid., 3.308, profiting from the translation of Atkinson and Sikes, in Machiavelli and correspondents, *Machiavelli and His Friends: Their Per-*

sonal Correspondence, ed. and trans. James B. Atkinson and David Sikes (DeKalb: University of Northern Illinois Press, 2004), 276.

36. Letter of Machiavelli, February 4, 1514, in *Opere,* 3.310.

37. Ibid.

38. Letter of Vettori, February 9, 1514, in *Opere,* 2.312.

39. Joanne Ferraro, *Marriage Wars in Late Renaissance Venice* (Oxford: Oxford University Press, 2001).

40. See Diana Robin, *Publishing Women: Salons, the Presses, and the Counter-Reformation in Sixteenth-Century Italy* (Chicago: University of Chicago Press, 2007); Virginia Cox, *The Prodigious Muse: Women's Writing in Counter-Reformation Italy* (Baltimore: Johns Hopkins University Press, 2011); Cox, *Women's Writing in Italy, 1400–1650* (Baltimore: Johns Hopkins University Press, 2008).

41. Vasari, *Vita di Domenico Puligo,* in Giorgio Vasari, *Le opere di Giorgio Vasari,* 9 vols., ed. Gaetano Milanesi (Florence: Sansoni, 1878–1885), 4:461–468, at 465.

42. Letter of Francesco Guicciardini, August 7, 1525, in *Opere,* 2.398.

43. Ibid.

44. Letter of Machiavelli, October 16–20, 1525, in *Opere,* 2.408.

45. *Clizia,* in *Opere,* 3.232.

46. Ibid., 3.233.

47. Ibid.

7. History

1. *Art of War,* in Niccolò Machiavelli, *Opere,* 3 vols., ed. Corrado Vivanti (Turin: Einaudi-Galimard, 1997–2005), 1.535.

2. See Marino Sanuto the Younger, *I diarii di Marino Sanuto,* 58 vols., ed. Rinaldo Fulin (Venice: Visentini, 1879–1903), 24:90.

3. J. N. Stephens, *The Fall of the Florentine Republic, 1512–1530* (Oxford: Oxford University Press, 1983), 108–109.

4. Jacopo Nardi, *Istorie della città di Firenze,* 2 vols. (Florence: Le Monnier, 1858), 2.61 and 2.63. See also Roberto Ridolfi, *The Life of Niccolò Machiavelli,* trans. Cecil Grayson (London: Routledge, 1963; reprint, Hoboken, N.J.: Taylor and Francis, 2013), 177.

5. *Art of War,* 6, in *Opere,* 1.644.

6. *Art of War*, 6, in *Opere*, 1.655.

7. *Art of War*, 7, in *Opere*, 1.689.

8. Christopher Lynch, "Introduction," in Niccolò Machiavelli, *Art of War*, ed. and trans. Christopher Lynch (Chicago: University of Chicago Press, 2003), xiii–xxxviii, at xxvi.

9. See Ridolfi, *The Life of Niccolò Machiavelli*, 182.

10. *Opere*, 1.733–745.

11. *Histories*, "Proemio," in *Opere*, 3.308.

12. *Histories*, "Proemio," in *Opere*, 3.309.

13. *Histories*, 5, in *Opere*, 3.519.

14. Ibid.

15. Ibid.

16. *Histories*, 1.5, in *Opere*, 3.318.

17. *Histories*, 1.5, in *Opere*, 3.319.

18. Ibid.

19. *Histories*, 1.9, in *Opere*, 3.325.

20. *Prince*, 11, in *Opere*, 1.147–148.

21. *Histories*, 1.23, in *Opere*, 3.341–342.

22. *Histories*, 3.1, in *Opere*, 3.423.

23. Ibid.

24. Ibid.

25. *Histories*, 3.1, in *Opere*, 3.424.

26. *Histories*, 7.1, in *Opere*, 3.629.

27. Ibid.

28. Juvenal, *Saturae*, in *A. Persi Flacci et D. Iuni Iuuenalis* Saturae, ed. W. V. Clausen (Oxford: Oxford University Press, 1992), 10.81.

29. *Histories*, 7.2, in *Opere*, 6.630.

30. Ibid.

31. *Histories*, 7.5, in *Opere*, 3.634.

32. Ibid.

33. Ibid.

34. Ibid.

35. *Histories*, 7.5, in *Opere*, 3.635.

36. Ibid.

37. Ibid.

38. *Discourses*, 1.12, in *Opere*, 1.231.

39. *Histories*, 8.36, in *Opere*, 3.730.
40. Ibid.
41. Ibid.
42. Ibid.
43. Ibid.

8. Ghosts

1. As Robert Black has related, the story regarding the dream was "first related by a French Jesuit, Étienne Binet"; see Robert Black, *Machiavelli* (London: Routledge, 2013), chap. 11; see there for an excellent survey of the available evidence concerning Machiavelli's death. For the deathbed confession see Giuliano Procacci, *Machiavelli nella cultura europea* (Rome: Laterza, 1995), 423–431, cited in William J. Connell, "Introduction," in Machiavelli, *The Prince, with Related Documents*, ed. and trans. William J. Connell (New York: Bedford/St. Martin's, 2005), 1–34, at 34n20.

2. Livy, *Ab urbe condita*, books 1–5, ed. Robert M. Ogilvie (Oxford: Oxford University Press, 1974), Praefatio.

3. Francesco Guicciardini, Maxim 28, cited by Alison Brown in Francesco Guicciardini, *Dialogue on the Government of Florence*, ed. and trans. Alison Brown (Cambridge: Cambridge University Press, 1994), 171.

4. Isaiah Berlin, *Against the Current*, 2nd ed., ed. Henry Hardy, introduction by Roger Hausheer, foreword by Mark Lilla (Princeton, N.J.: Princeton University Press, 2013), 33–100.

5. *Discourses*, 1.4, in Niccolò Machiavelli, *Opere*, 3 vols., ed. Corrado Vivanti (Turin: Einaudi-Galimard, 1997–2005), 1.209.

6. Ibid.

7. Ibid., 1.210.

8. Ibid., alluding to Cicero, *On Friendship*, 25, 95.

9. This commonplace was attributed to Cato the Elder by Quintilian in his *Institutio oratoria*, ed. Michael Winterbottom, 2 vols. (Oxford: Oxford University Press, 1970), 12.1.

10. *Prince*, 3, in *Opere*, 1.123.

11. Ibid., 1.124.

12. *Histories*, 7, in *Opere*, 3.635.

13. *Discourses*, 3.30, in *Opere*, 1.492.

14. *Discourses*, 1.12, in *Opere*, 1.231.

15. See J. G. A. Pocock, *The Machiavellian Moment: Florentine Republican Thought and the Atlantic Republican Tradition* (Princeton, N.J.: Princeton University Press, 1975, reissued with a new afterword by the author, 2003).

16. Letter of Machiavelli to Guicciardini, in *Opere*, 2.408–411, at 411.

Bibliography

Note on sources: All translations from Machiavelli are my own, though I have benefited from the English versions of his works included here. Citations to Machiavelli's works are to the three-volume edition of Corrado Vivanti, abbreviated as *Opere*.

Anglo, Sydney. *Machiavelli: The First Century*. Oxford: Oxford University Press, 2005.

Aristotle. *Politica*. Edited by David Ross. Oxford: Oxford University Press, 1957.

Aulus Gellius. *Noctes atticae*. Edited by P. K. Marshall. Oxford: Oxford University Press, 1990.

Bacon, Francis. *The Advancement of Learning*. Edited by William A. Wright. Oxford: Clarendon, 1880.

Bell, David. *The First Total War: Napoleon's Europe and the Birth of Warfare as We Know It*. New York: Houghton Mifflin, 2007.

Benes, Carrie. *Urban Legends: Civic Identity and the Classical Past in Northern Italy, 1250–1350*. State College: Pennsylvania State University Press, 2011.

Berlin, Isaiah. *Against the Current*. 2nd ed. Edited by Henry Hardy, introduction by Roger Hausheer, foreword by Mark Lilla. Princeton, N.J.: Princeton University Press, 2013.

Bertelli, Sergio, and Franco Gaeta. "Noterelle Machiavelliane: Un codice di Lucrezio e di Terenzio." *Rivista storica italiana* 73 (1961): 544–555.

Billanovich, Giuseppe. *La tradizione del testo di Livio e le origini dell'umanesimo*. 2 vols. Padua: Antenore, 1981.

Black, Robert. *Machiavelli*. London: Routledge, 2013.

Bracciolini, Poggio. *On Avarice*. Translated by Benjamin Kohl and Elizabeth B. Welles. In *The Earthly Republic*, edited by Benjamin Kohl
and Ronald G. Witt, 241–289. Philadelphia: University of Pennsylvania Press, 1978.

Brown, Alison. *The Return of Lucretius to Renaissance Florence*. Cambridge,
Mass.: Harvard University Press, 2010.

Burckhardt, Jacob. *The Civilization of the Renaissance in Italy*. Translated
by S. C. J. Middlemore. London: Kegan Paul and Co., 1878.

———. *Die Cultur der Renaissance in Italien: Ein Versuch*. Basel:
Schweighauser, 1960.

Castiglionchio the Younger, Lapo da. "On the Benefits of the Papal Court."
In Christopher S. Celenza, *Renaissance Humanism and the Papal
Curia: Lapo da Castiglionchio the Younger's* De curiae commodis,
102–227. Ann Arbor: University of Michigan Press, 1999.

Celenza, Christopher S. "End Game: Humanist Latin in the Late Fifteenth
Century." In *Latinitas Perennis II: Appropriation and Latin Litera-
ture*, edited by Y. Maes, J. Papy, and W. Verbaal, 201–242. Leiden:
Brill, 2009.

———. "Late Antiquity and the Italian Renaissance." In *The Oxford
Handbook of Late Antiquity*, edited by S. F. Johnson, 1172–1199. Oxford: Oxford University Press, 2012.

Cerretani, Bartolomeo. *Storia fiorentina*. Edited by G. Berti. Florence:
Olschki, 1994.

Connell, William J. "Introduction." In *Machiavelli, The Prince, with Related
Documents*, edited and translated by William J. Connell, 1–34.
New York: Bedford/St. Martin's, 2005.

———. "La lettera di Machiavelli a Vettori del 10 dicembre 1513." *Archivio
storico italiano* 171 (2013): 665–723.

———. "New Light on Machiavelli's letter to Vettori, 10 December 1513."
In *Europe e Italia, Studi in onore di Giorgio Chittolini / Europe and
Italy, Studies in Honor of Giorgio Chittolini*. Florence: Florence Uni-
versity Press, 2011, 93–127.

Cooper, Roslyn Pesman. "Machiavelli, Francesco Soderini, and don Michelotto." *Nuova rivista storica* 66 (1982): 342–357.

Cox, Virginia. *The Prodigious Muse: Women's Writing in Counter-
Reformation Italy*. Baltimore: Johns Hopkins University Press, 2011.

————. *Women's Writing in Italy, 1400–1650.* Baltimore: Johns Hopkins University Press, 2008.

Dante Alighieri. *Comedia.* Edited by Federico Sanguineti. Florence: Edizioni del Galluzzo, 2001.

D'Elia, Anthony F. *A Sudden Terror: The Plot to Murder the Pope in Renaissance Rome.* Cambridge, Mass.: Harvard University Press, 2009.

Fachard, Denis, ed. *Consulte e pratiche della Repubblica fiorentina, 1505–1512.* Geneva: Droz, 1988.

Ferraro, Joanne. *Marriage Wars in Late Renaissance Venice.* Oxford: Oxford University Press, 2001.

Finch, Chauncey E. "Machiavelli's Copy of Lucretius." *Classical Journal* 56 (1960): 29–32.

Gouwens, Kenneth, and Sheryl E. Reiss, eds. *The Pontificate of Clement VII: Politics, History, Culture.* Aldershot: Ashgate, 2005.

Greenblatt, Stephen. *The Swerve: How the World Became Modern.* New York: Norton, 2013.

Guicciardini, Francesco. *Dialogue on the Government of Florence.* Edited and translated by Alison Brown. Cambridge: Cambridge University Press, 1994.

Hankins, James, ed. *Renaissance Civic Humanism: Reappraisals and Reflections.* Cambridge: Cambridge University Press, 2000.

Hobbins, Daniel. *Authorship and Publicity before Print: Jean Gerson and the Transformation of late Medieval Learning.* Philadelphia: University of Pennsylvania Press, 2009.

Hörnquist, Mikael. "Perché non si usa allegare i Romani: Machiavelli and the Florentine Militia of 1506." *Renaissance Quarterly* 55 (2002): 148–191.

————. "The Two Myths of Civic Humanism." In *Renaissance Civic Humanism: Reappraisals and Reflections,* edited by James Hankins, 105–142. Cambridge: Cambridge University Press, 2000.

Juvenal. *Saturae,* 35–198, in *A. Persi Flacci et D. Iuni Iuuenalis Saturae,* edited by W. V. Clausen. Oxford: Oxford University Press, 1992.

Kent, F. William. *Lorenzo de' Medici and the Art of Magnificence.* Baltimore: Johns Hopkins University Press, 2004.

Kohl, Benjamin, and Ronald G. Witt, eds. *The Earthly Republic.* Philadelphia: University of Pennsylvania Press, 1978.

Landino, Cristoforo. "Orazione fatta per Cristofano da Pratovecchio quando cominciò a leggere i sonnetti di messer Francesco Petrarca in istudio." In *La critica del Landino,* edited by Roberto Cardini, 342–354. Florence: Sansoni, 1973.

Landucci, Luca. *Diario fiorentino dal 1450 al 1516.* Florence: Biblos, 1969.

Livy. *Ab urbe condita,* books 1–5. Edited by Robert M. Ogilvie. Oxford: Oxford University Press, 1974.

———. *Ab urbe condita,* books 6–10. Edited by R. S. Conway and C. F. Walters. Oxford: Oxford University Press, 1963.

Lucretius. *De Rerum Natura.* Edited by Cyril Bailey. Oxford: Oxford University Press, 1922.

Lynch, Christopher. "Introduction." In Niccolò Machiavelli, *Art of War,* edited and translated by Christopher Lynch, xiii–xxxviii. Chicago: University of Chicago Press, 2003.

Machiavelli, Bernardo. *Ricordi.* Edited by Leonardo Olschki. Florence: Le Monnier, 1954.

Machiavelli, Niccolò. *Art of War.* Edited and translated by Christopher Lynch. Chicago: University of Chicago Press, 2003.

———. *Mandragola.* In *Five Comedies from the Italian Renaissance,* edited and translated by Laura Giannetti and Guido Ruggiero, 71–116. Baltimore: Johns Hopkins University Press, 2003.

———. *Opere.* 3 vols. Edited by Corrado Vivanti. Turin: Einaudi-Galimard, 1997–2005.

———. *The Prince, with Related Documents.* Edited and translated by William J. Connell. New York: Bedford/St. Martin's, 2005.

———. *De principatibus.* Edited by Giorgio Inglese. Rome: Nella sede dell'Istituto, 1994.

———. *Il principe.* Edited by Giorgio Inglese. Turin: Einaudi, 1995.

Machiavelli, Niccolò, and correspondents. *Machiavelli and His Friends: Their Personal Correspondence.* Edited and translated by James B. Atkinson and David Sikes. DeKalb: University of Northern Illinois Press, 2004.

Mansfield, Harvey. *Machiavelli's New Modes and Orders: A Study on the Discourses on Livy.* Chicago: University of Chicago Press, 2001.

Martines, Lauro. *April Blood: Florence and the Plot against the Medici.* Oxford: Oxford University Press, 2003.

————. *Fire in the City: Savonarola and the Struggle for the Soul of Florence*. Oxford: Oxford University Press, 2006.

Masters, Roger D. *Fortune Is a River: Leonardo da Vinci and Machiavelli's Magnificent Dream to Change the Course of Florentine History*. New York: Free Press, 1998.

Medici, Lorenzo de'. *Canti carnascialeschi*. Edited by Paolo Orvieto. Rome: Salerno editrice, 1991.

Milner, Stephen J. "'Fanno bandire, notificare, et expressamente comandare': Town Criers and the Information Economy of Renaissance Florence." *I Tatti Studies in the Italian Renaissance* 16 (2013): 107–151.

Najemy, John M. *Between Friends: Discourses of Power and Desire in the Machiavelli-Vettori Letters of 1513–1515*. Princeton, N.J.: Princeton University Press, 1993.

————, ed. *The Cambridge Companion to Machiavelli*. Cambridge: Cambridge University Press, 2010.

————. "Introduction." In *The Cambridge Companion to Machiavelli*, edited by John M. Najemy, 1–13. Cambridge: Cambridge University Press, 2010.

Nardi, Jacopo. *Istorie della città di Firenze*. 2 vols. Florence: Le Monnier, 1858.

Nerli, Filippo de'. *Commentari de' fatti civili occursi dentro la città di Firenze dall'anno 1215 al 1537*. Augsburg: Mertz and Mayer, 1728.

Osmond, Patricia J. "The Conspiracy of 1522 against Cardinal Giulio de' Medici: Machiavelli and *gli esempli degli antiqui*." In *The Pontificate of Clement VII: Politics, History, Culture*, edited by K. Gouwens and S. E. Reiss, 55–72. Aldershot: Ashgate, 2005.

Palmer, Ada. *Reading Lucretius in the Renaissance*. Cambridge, Mass.: Harvard University Press, 2014.

Passanante, Gerard. *The Lucretian Renaissance: Philology and the Afterlife of Tradition*. Chicago: University of Chicago Press, 2011.

Petrarca (Petrarch), Francesco. *Canzoniere*. Edited by Roberto Antonelli. Turin: Einaudi, 1992.

————. *Le familiari / Rerum familiarum libri*. 4 vols. Edited by Vittorio Rossi. Florence: Le Lettere, 1997.

Pliny the Younger. *Epistularum libri decem*. Edited by Roger Mynors. Oxford: Oxford University Press, 1963.

Pocock, J. G. A. *The Machiavellian Moment: Florentine Republican Thought and the Atlantic Republican Tradition*. Princeton, N.J.: Princeton University Press, 1975. Reissued with a new afterword by the author, 2003.

Poliziano, Angelo. "Commentary on the Pazzi Conspiracy." Translated by Elizabeth B. Welles. In *The Earthly Republic*, edited by Benjamin Kohl and Ronald G. Witt, 305–324. Philadelphia: University of Pennsylvania Press, 1978.

Procacci, Giuliano. *Machiavelli nella cultura europea*. Rome: Laterza, 1995.

Quintilian. *Institutio oratoria*. 2 vols. Edited by Michael Winterbottom. Oxford: Oxford University Press, 1970.

Ridolfi, Roberto. *The Life of Niccolò Machiavelli*. Translated by Cecil Grayson. London: Routledge, 1963. Reprint, Hoboken, N.J.: Taylor and Francis, 2013.

Robin, Diana. *Publishing Women: Salons, the Presses, and the Counter-Reformation in Sixteenth-Century Italy*. Chicago: University of Chicago Press, 2007.

Rocke, Michael. *Forbidden Friendships: Homosexuality and Male Culture in Renaissance Florence*. Oxford: Oxford University Press, 1996.

Ruggiero, Guido. *Machiavelli in Love: Sex, Self, and Society in the Italian Renaissance*. Baltimore: Johns Hopkins University Press, 2007.

Sanuto, Marino, the Younger. *I diarii di Marino Sanuto*. 58 vols. Edited by Rinaldo Fulin. Venice: Visentini, 1879–1903.

Stephens, J. N. *The Fall of the Florentine Republic, 1512–1530*. Oxford: Oxford University Press, 1983.

Tacitus. *Annalium ab excessu divi Augusti libri*. Edited by Charles D. Fisher. Oxford: Oxford University Press, 1906.

Vasari, Giorgio. *Le opere di Giorgio Vasari*. 9 vols. Edited by Gaetano Milanesi. Florence: Sansoni, 1878–1885.

Virgil. *P. Vergili Maronis Opera*. Edited by R. A. B. Mynors. Oxford: Oxford University Press, 1969.

Viroli, Maurizio. *Redeeming* The Prince: *The Meaning of Machiavelli's Masterpiece*. Princeton, N.J.: Princeton University Press, 2013.

Weinstein, Donald. *Savonarola: The Rise and Fall of a Renaissance Prophet*. New Haven, Conn.: Yale University Press, 2011.

Whitfield, J. H. "Machiavelli's Use of Livy." In *Livy*, edited by T. A. Dorey, 73–96. London: Routledge, 1971.

Acknowledgments

Many thanks to Francesco Borghesi, whose 2013 invitation to the University of Sydney led me to write this book. Presenting a public lecture there on Machiavelli's *Prince* led me to think more generally about Machiavelli, and the genial and stimulating discussions in Sydney remain with me to this day.

I wrote the book, for the most part, while serving as director of the American Academy in Rome, a position I held from 2010 to 2014. The constant intellectual stimulation I enjoyed at the Academy was unparalleled. To Adele Chatfield-Taylor and Mark Robbins, the two presidents of that institution under whom I served, thank you. And to my Rome colleagues, especially Corey Brennan, Karl Kirchwey, Kim Bowes, Peter Miller, and Sebastian Hierl, thank you for opening up intellectual and creative worlds about which I never would have known. To Marina Lella, *grazie infinite* for all you did during those years. Finally, it is to the community of the Academy itself—the fellows, residents, affiliated fellows, and visitors—that I owe the greatest debt. It would be impossible to list the thousands of people who passed through the Academy during my time there. But encountering the richness that emerges when artists and scholars live and work together permitted me, at the very least, to see my academic work in a new light, as one voice in a vast polyphony. It made me believe that explanation of specialized subjects was possible, indeed necessary, across different fields of endeavor.

A book written for general audiences depends on specialized work done by scholars past and present. Two such scholars, Stephen J. Milner and William J. Connell, whose work I admire greatly, offered help at crucial moments. The two anonymous readers for Harvard University Press offered innumerable improvements.

As to Machiavelli, he is that rare figure who has something new to say to each generation. And there is no shortage of good books on Machiavelli. So thanks most of all to Lindsay Waters, the commissioning editor of this book, for believing in the project.

To the book's dedicatee, Anna Harwell Celenza, words could never do justice. So I will leave it at a simple "thank you," for everything.

Index